PATHMASTER GUIDES

CIRCULAR
30 WALKS FROM REGIONAL CENTRES

THE AUVERGNE

Maurice Turner

Series Editor
Richard Sale

The Crowood Press

First published in 1992 by
The Crowood Press Ltd
Ramsbury
Marlborough
Wiltshire SN8 2HR

British Library Cataloguing in Publication Data
A catalogue record for this book is
available from the British Library

Picture credits
Black and white photographs throughout, and cover photographs by the author; all maps by Malcolm Walker.

In places times from timetables and certain costs, including fares, have been quoted. These were correct at time of going to press, but it cannot be guaranteed that they will remain the same in subsequent years.

Printed and bound in Great Britain by
BPCC Hazells Ltd
Member of BPCC Ltd

CONTENTS

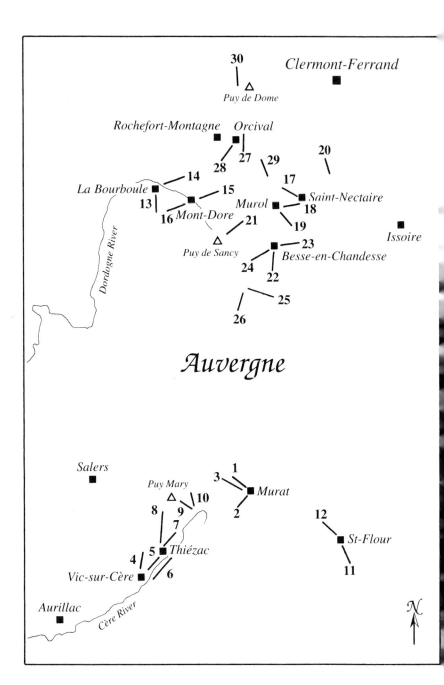

30

Clermont-Ferrand ■

Puy de Dome △

Rochefort-Montagne ■   Orcival ■

28   27   29   20

La Bourboule ■   14   17   Saint-Nectaire ■

13   15   Murol ■   18

16   Mont-Dore   21   19

Dordogne River

Puy de Sancy △

23

24   Besse-en-Chandesse

22   Issoire ■

25

26

Auvergne

Salers ■   1

Puy Mary △   3

8   9   10   Murat ■

7   2

12   St-Flour ■

4   5   Thiézac ■

Vic-sur-Cère ■   6   11

Aurillac ■   Cère River

N

4

INTRODUCTION

The Auvergne as a Walking Area

The mountains of the Auvergne are undoubtedly one of the more popular walking areas of France, though with so many other good areas available they are certainly not over exploited. The reasons for their popularity are not hard to find: their beauty is well known, to the French at least, and access to the mountains has been made easy by local groups who have worked very hard to ensure that paths are kept open and are clearly waymarked. The result is a fine network of footpaths, with something for walkers of all abilities – short rambles, more arduous scrambles, and long, demanding cross-country routes.

Enjoyable footpaths can be found in all parts of the Auvergne, though, inevitably, the most heavily-used paths are those within easy travelling distance of the centres of population - and in the Auvergne travelling is not difficult. The creation of the regional *Parc des Volcans*, in 1977, reflected the public demand for access to this geologically-fascinating area, and tourism is well promoted in certain places. But the sheer size of the region ensures that it is always possible to get off the beaten track, and even at the height of the holiday season it is still possible to walk all day without meeting anyone else. Tourism has meant some places undergoing considerable change, but others retain ancient traditions and ways of life. In these there is much to see: châteaux, more modest houses, gardens, and the splendid Romanesque churches for which the Auvergne is renowned.

Neither is there any shortage of interesting natural objects. The volcanoes have a special fascination, but everywhere the volcanic rocks have weathered to create acidic soils supporting a diverse flora. Botanists will find plants that are rarities elsewhere growing quite prolifically, and the meadows in early summer are a riot of colour. Meadows full of white narcissi are a surprisingly common sight, where on higher slopes alpine daffodils – especially the Alpine Lent Lily – appear in abundance.

Even more welcome to the visitor with an interest in the natural environment is the prevalence of large birds of prey, such as the buzzards, kites, and peregrine falcons. The eagle owl can also be seen, though the golden eagle is unaccountably absent.

The development of tourism has transformed the almost-legendary difficulties of access to some parts of the Auvergne. Although few new roads have been created, and only at Clermont-Ferrand is there an autoroute crossing the region, there has been a policy of upgrading all the principal routes in recent years, and these are now of a high standard. Some of the major roads have regular bus services, but in general the visitor using public transport is far better served by rural rail services. This has been borne in mind in planning the walks, for although they all return the walker to the starting point, they have been chosen so as to be accessible – wherever possible – by both road and rail.

Before turning to the centres themselves, it is necessary to explain just what is included in the area known as the Auvergne. Originally the term was used to describe the territory of a Gaulish tribe, the *Averni*, and has sometimes been used in an equally broad sense to refer to the whole of the central uplands. The modern planning region of Auvergne, on the other hand, consists only of the *départements* of Allier, Puy de Dôme, and Cantal. Some geographers restrict the use of the term even more, limiting it to the line of volcanic hills and mountains extending from Volvic in the north to the Cère valley in the south. This was the usage adopted in naming the regional park, the *Parc des Volcans d'Auvergne*, and in fact the walks described here nearly all lie within that park.

It may be as well to mention at this point that French policy with regard to Regional Parks differs in some respects from that adopted elsewhere. The policy results from the relatively low population density of the Massif Central, and the fact that so much of it is devoted to forestry, a combination of rising costs and poor returns having forced many small farmers to move out, abandoning much of the marginal land. In recent years French policy has been actively to encourage hill farmers to stay, in order to maintain the traditional way of life, while discouraging or even forbidding commercial forestry. As a result, clear felling followed by replanting is exceptional, and the traditional mixed broadleaf and coniferous forests are managed to the minimum extent, being left to regenerate naturally after thinning.

How to Get There

By *air*

The only airport in the region is at Clermont-Ferrand, which has regular services to and from Paris, Lyon, Bordeaux, Toulouse, Marseille, and Nice.

There is an efficient 10 minute shuttle service between the airport and the SNCF railway station in Clermont-Ferrand. International flights are much less frequent, however, and, unless you are fortunate enough to find a convenient one, it may be better to fly to Paris and then transfer to an internal flight, or to travel on by rail.

By rail

Clermont-Ferrand is also the key to rail services in the northern Auvergne and can be reached in less than four hours by regular services from the Gare de Lyon in Paris. There is no motorail facility. By changing trains, the mountains of the Chaîne des Puys can be reached by using the line from Clermont towards Ussel-Brive, but if travelling to La Bourboule or Le Mont-Dore it is necessary to make a further connection (for which no waiting is involved) at Laqueuille. Cantal, on the other hand, can be reached more easily by making use of the service from Paris – Austerlitz station via Limoges to Brive. This also takes around four hours. At Brive you can change for Aurillac and the branch line towards Murat. Alternatively, since Brive has the advantage of being a motorail terminal, you can easily drive to Cantal using your own car.

A point worth considering if you are travelling by rail is that possession of a national Railcard may entitle you to buy a low cost European Railcard, with considerable savings on rail journeys in France.

By road

During the summer season (roughly June to September inclusive), there are three coaches each day making the 90 minute journey from Clermont railway station to Besse-en-Chandesse. Similar coaches (details available from local tourist offices) serve Saint-Nectaire and other centres east of the Sancy massif which are not accessible by rail. Alternatively car hire can be easily arranged from Clermont-Ferrand for the northern part of the region, or from Brive or Aurillac for the southern part.

French speed limits are: built-up areas 60 kms/hr; outside built-up areas 90 kms/hr; dual carriageways 110 kms/hr; autoroutes 130 kms/hr (reduced to 110 kms/hr on urban stretches and also reduced in wet weather). Those autoroutes marked as *péages* are subject to a toll, which can be expensive if you are travelling any distance – and particularly so if you are towing a caravan. Alternative routes are often of a high standard, and are not usually busy, though even small towns can sometimes take a long time to negotiate.

Children under the age of 10 are not permitted to travel as front seat passengers if rear seating is available. Although it is not compulsory to carry a fire extinguisher, first aid kit, and spare light bulbs in France, as it is in some other countries, it is still a wise precaution to have them. Petrol can invariably be obtained by credit card. Unleaded fuel (*sans plomb*) is now widely available, but is usually of the more expensive premium kind.

You will need to have with you your national driving licence, and vehicle registration document, as well as your passport.

In case of serious accident, telephone 18 for the fire service, and 17 for the police. They will inform the ambulance service, as there is no national call-out number, though the number of the local service should be displayed in the telephone box. In case of breakdown, you may be fortunate enough to find an emergency telephone, but do not count on it. France has no countrywide motoring club service, and a local garage is your best bet. They are required to display a list of their charges.

If for any reason, whether accident or breakdown, you are forced to stop on the road, you should note that hazard warning lights are not enough, but need to be supplemented by a warning triangle placed at a suitable distance. On an autoroute you should, of course, be able to get on to a hard shoulder, and in that event the police may organise assistance for you.

Terrain and Climate

Though the mountains of the Auvergne are the highest of the Massif Central, their height is still less than 2,000m, which is low even by Pyrenéean standards, much less those of the Alps. At the same time, their distance from the sea ensures a Continental climate, with great differences between summer and winter. The summers are hot and dry, but though there are days when the heat is overpowering, in general conditions are likely to be ideal for walking.

The plateau from which the mountains rise is typically about 1,000m above sea level, which makes it cooler than it would be at lower levels, while at the same time ensuring that there is not too much climbing to reach even the highest summits. The heavy winter rains – not to mention the heavy snowfalls sometimes experienced – allied to the moderate altitude results in a lush vegetation. This means that the ascents can often be made in the shade, which is a considerable benefit when compared to the treeless climbs sometimes necessary elsewhere.

The gradients moreover, are not too steep, for the valley sides of the

Chaîne des Puys, at least, are too young to have suffered extensive glaciation, and are much more likely to be V-shaped than U-shaped, with considerable advantage to the walker. The mountains of the Sancy massif and Cantal are rather steeper, but tend to be linked by ridges not much lower than the summits themselves, so that, once having arrived on a ridge, there is little more climbing and descending.

In common with mountain areas everywhere, the Auvergne is subject to sudden summer storms. Dry stream beds can become raging torrents in no time at all, and many walks show abundant evidence of the force of the floods, which have carried away roads and bridges not just once, but many times. Fortunately, you are likely to be aware of a storm in the offing well beforehand, and it is usually not too difficult to change your itinerary to suit.

Accommodation

The Auvergne has an impressive range of holiday accommodation on offer, and only a few very popular spots are fully booked – even at peak season. Unfortunately, very little is advertised outside France, so that the prospective walker is faced with a problem. The necessary information is readily available when you get there, at the *Syndicat d'Initiative* sited in every town and many villages, and this is fine if you are touring. But if your object is to do some walking, and you have decided on your centre, you do at least need to know that the kind of accommodation you prefer is likely to be available.

There is another dimension to this, too. The French holiday season is shorter than that of many other countries and is highly concentrated. This means that many of the facilities you might expect to find on holiday, hotels, restaurants, camp sites – even museums or swimming pools – may not be open until the middle of June, and may well close again in mid-September.

Fortunately a list covering hotels in the Auvergne, can be obtained by writing, enclosing a stamped and addressed envelope, to:

> Comité Régionale du Tourisme, 43 Avenue Julien,
> 63011 Clermont-Ferrand, France.

The introductory notes are in six languages, including English, which makes clear the commitment to attract foreign tourists. The notes explain the star rating system for French hotels, while the list itself, covering the *départements* of Allier, Cantal, Haute-Loire, and Puy de Dôme, gives all the information needed. Hotels are listed in alphabetical order by the name of the town or village, which is fine for all the centres from which walks are described here, but it does mean that since there is no map, hotels in obscure villages nearby can easily be missed.

Better organised is the list of farm accommodation available from:

> Chambre Régionale d'Agriculture, 43 Avenue Julien,
> 63012 Clermont-Ferrand, France.

This includes temporary camp sites (*camping – caravanning a la ferme*): guesthouses and farmhouses (*chambres d'hôtes, fermes de séjour, fermes auberges, auberges de campagne, or fermes equestre*). The area covered is as for the hotels, but in this case the information is listed by *département*, and there is a map. There is also a brief description, in English, of local facilities accompanying each entry. The only fault with this excellent brochure, in fact, is its extreme brevity, with only a handful of entries in each category.

This criticism hardly applies to the next publication, which comprises 127 commercial or municipal camp sites (together with sundry *autres campings*) in Puy de Dôme alone. It is available from:

> Comité Departemental de Tourisme du Puy de Dôme,
> 17 Place Delille, 63038 Clermont-Ferrand, France.

As with the hotels, star ratings are given, and the system is fully explained. Each site is illustrated, and there is also a map.

Of particular interest to walkers are the *Gîtes d'Etape*, which follow the original youth hostel tradition of catering only for those travelling under their own steam, and limit each stay to two consecutive nights. They sometimes have a warden, but usually not, and are situated almost exclusively on *Grande Randonnée* – the long distance footpath network. A list of the available *Gîtes* in Puy de Dôme can be obtained from the same address as that given for camp sites in the last paragraph.

Finally, Gîtes de France is an organisation which arranges the letting of holiday cottages throughout France on behalf of their owners. They will also book ferries and overnight accommodation in hotels en route to the *Gîtes*. For those travelling by car, there can be little doubt that this is an easy and convenient way of arranging a holiday in France. Gîtes de France provide a comprehensive illustrated guide to all the cottages, arranged by regions, and giving all the necessary details. The address to write to is:

> Gîtes de France Ltd.
> 178 Piccadilly, London W1V 9DB

but it is worth noting that much of this accommodation for the months of July and August is already booked up by the New Year.

Transport

Within Auvergne, as defined by the Regional Park, those parts of greatest scenic beauty are served by three railway lines and a few major roads. In the north, both the volcanic peaks centred on Puy de Dôme and the glaciated summits of Les Monts Dore are made accessible by the railway line from Clermont-Ferrand to the town of Le Mont-Dore; by the D941 road from Riom to Pontgibaud; and by the D941a, D941b, and N89, all of which radiate from Clermont-Ferrand.

In the south of the region, the mountains of Cantal can be conveniently reached by a frequent rail service from Murat to Aurillac (which connects with the main line at Brive), and since the branch line is accompanied throughout its length by a trunk road, the N122, the walks described here start from those places served by both means of transport. Finally, there is a third rail link which goes from Murat by way of the junction at Neussargues-Moissac either to Saint-Flour, or north to Riom-es-Montagnes and Bort-les-Orgues. This final branch has rather less frequent services, which makes it less useful for day-to-day use, but permits visitors to reach popular walking centres providing accommodation.

Money

The French unit of currency is the franc. Getting money changed is easy – once you have found a bank that is open. But banks are rarely available in the villages and, unless your hotel is prepared to cash a cheque for you, a special visit to the nearest town, at a time when the bank will be open, may be called for. This might not, of course, fit in with your other plans, particularly as you may well find that the bank opens only on certain days of the week.

For all these reasons, you will probably find it necessary to keep a reasonable sum of French money in hand. There is no limit to the currency you can take into France, though there are restrictions on bringing out large amounts of money in cash. The remainder of your money can conveniently and safely be kept in the form of traveller's cheques or Eurocheques. The situation relating to the use of credit cards is changing, and in the larger towns you will not find any difficulty in using Access, Visa, or American Express at hotels, restaurants, and filling stations (though they are not accepted at supermarkets). The practice does not seem to have spread to smaller towns and villages yet, and there francs are still the only acceptable currency.

The Law for Walkers

The French attitude to walkers is in some respects different from that of other nations. Their paths are rarely legally-designated rights of way, but, because those in the Auvergne are not over-used, there is hardly ever any opposition by farmers to the use of paths by walkers, nor is there any real distinction other than that of practicability, between footpaths and bridleways. The situation is not quite as good in urban areas, or where there has been large-scale conversion of farms into holiday homes, but this is an unusual state of affairs in Auvergne. It goes without saying that walkers should observe common courtesies, and obey the *Code du Randonneur* reproduced below.

The walks described here make use of three different kinds of path. The Auvergne is crossed by a number of *Grande Randonnée*, or long-distance footpaths, similar to those found elsewhere, and short sections of these have been utilised where convenient. They are designated by G R numbers rather than names, and are waymarked in red and white. Other walks, or parts of them, make use of the *Petite Randonnée* which are usually, though not invariably, circular walks and are waymarked – and cleared when necessary – by local groups. When the route consists of no more than a faint line – through forests, particularly – waymarks can be invaluable. But when several routes make use of the same line, the resulting waymarks can be all the colours of the rainbow, and simply confuse what is very often a perfectly straightforward path. For this reason I have omitted to mention waymarks unless they fulfil a useful purpose, and are not likely to create doubt.

Where neither exist, other footpaths marked on the map have been used. Sometimes these have proved to be impassable, farm tracks or minor roads have been pressed into service. These suffer neither from difficulties of access nor an excess of traffic.

Just occasionally – and this really only applies to a very small minority of tracks, and even then only on weekends or public holidays – you may find the peace and quiet shattered by a noisy procession of four-wheel drive vehicles, heading over the mountains on heavily-rutted tracks. Where this is a possibility I have mentioned the fact, but in the *Parc des Volcans* they are trying very hard to reduce the nuisance, and you will see lots of notices discouraging drivers from this practice.

The *Code du Randonneur*

1. Love and respect nature.
2. Avoid unnecessary noise.
3. Destroy nothing.
4. Leave no litter.
5. Do not pick flowers or plants.
6. Do not disturb wildlife.
7. Close all gates.
8. Protect and preserve the environment.
9. No smoking or fires in the forests.
10. Keep to the footpath.
11. Respect the country way of life and the country people.
12. Think of others as you would think of yourself.

The only parts of the code which require any comment are items 5 and 9. Picking of wild flowers is flagrantly practised by some French walkers, but in criticising them we should remember that, due to the sparing use of pesticides in the Auvergne, their meadows have not suffered to the same extent as elsewhere, and to them it does not seem such a crime. The danger of forest fires, on the other hand, is frequently brought home to them, and as a result this rule is actively enforced by both foresters an police.

Clothing and Equipment

Your needs are likely to be dictated much more by the weather than by any other factor. The mountains of the Auvergne have a fearsome reputation for snow in winter – which has been noticeable by its absence in recent years – but no walker worth his salt would go on the high ridges in winter without the full range of mountain equipment. The vast majority of walkers will, however, be visiting the region in summer, and it is to them that the following advice is directed.

In June, July, August and September it is almost certain to be hot, and probably very hot, in the valleys. Unless you are used to these temperatures it is sensible to wear a hat and to keep your neck covered. Other than that, you will probably wear what everyone else is wearing – shorts and a tee-shirt. For low level walking most people these days wear trainers with loop-stitched socks, and they seem to be quite adequate. In case of the occasional storm, it is as well to be prepared by carrying a cagoule, but the most essential thing to pack in your rucksack is plenty of liquid. Even in the valleys, not every village has a cafe, or even a bar, though its public water supply may be marked to reassure you that it is safe to drink.

On the mountains footwear, particularly, needs a bit more thought. Lightweight boots are very little heavier than trainers and, personally, I think they are worth their weight in gold when the paths are steep and rough. It is not just a matter of grip, but of ankle support. In addition, the light will be that bit brighter at higher altitudes, and you may need sunglasses. The sun may still be hot, increasing the risk of sunburn, but there will certainly be more of a breeze, and you may need to put on an extra layer when you stop.

On relatively empty mountains like those of the Auvergne, you cannot rely on meeting anyone else if things go wrong, so you do need to carry a first aid kit, some emergency food and a copious supply of liquid. A large scale map and a compass are absolutely essential, as is the ability to use them.

But, the probability is that you will experience nothing but clear skies and perfect visibility, and will wonder why all the precautions were necessary.

Food and Wine

The Auvergne is not famed for its cooking, but it is known throughout France for its *charcuteries* and its cheeses. The word *charcuterie* originally described a pork butcher's shop selling raw and cooked pork in the form of sausage, terrine, and pâté, though nowadays they also sell prepared meat dishes. Each village used to produce its own variation, and many of these are still made and sold locally. The Auvergne dish known as *fricandeau*, for example, is a pork pâté wrapped in salt pork, *Friand de Saint-Flour* is a sausage meat pâté wrapped in pastry, still sold in that town, while *saucisson brioche* is sausages-in-batter, French-style toad-in-the-hole.

Potato dishes, traditionally eaten by the peasants, are still popular. *Truffade au jambon de pays*, which consists of grilled mashed potatoes with grated cheese and ham, while *potée Auvergnate*, contains salt pork, potatoes, sausage and cabbage. Cabbage was always a widely-used vegetable and sometimes appears in unlikely combinations, the unlikeliest being *truite braisée aux choux*, braised trout with cabbage.

Trout very often appears on the menu, reflecting lower prices resulting from widespread fish farming, and is often offered with a cheese sauce. Cheese is, of course, the other item for which the Auvergne has acquired a reputation. Indeed, it has sometimes been called the cheese-board of France. In addition to its use in cooking (*poulet au fromage*, for instance, and *truite au fromage*)

Auvergne blue, in particular, is found with walnuts in salads (*salade au bleu et aux noix*), and the cheese board usually includes all the local varieties.

The best known of these are Cantal, which is not unlike Cheddar, and Saint-Nectaire, a soft cheese made from very fresh milk, which is ripened in damp cellars on rye-straw. Not surprisingly, in view of the importance of fresh milk, the best Saint-Nectaire is home-made on specialist farms such as Les Planchettes near Orcival. A similar cheese with a hole in the middle and a pink rind takes the name of Murol, a village only a short distance from Saint-Nectaire. Goat's milk and ewe's milk cheeses are also made in this area, though they are not as popular. Bleu d'Auvergne is now invariably factory-made but one of its best variants, *bleu de Thiézac*, is still made on farms in the vicinity of the village. It is said to be especially good between June and November.

Of the wines of Auvergne only Saint-Pourçain and Côtes d'Auvergne are known outside the immediate locality. Four communes only, Clermont-Chantargue, Coret, Chateaugay, and Riom-Madargue, are allowed to use the Côtes d'Auvergne appellation. These light red wines are said to have improved greatly in recent years, being not unlike Beaujolais. The dry whites of Saint-Pourçain, on the other hand, have been more highly regarded for a considerable time. They are at their best when young, and do not travel well.

It is widely believed that the volcanic soils of the Auvergne impart a special flavour to fruit and other products, and this reputation may have helped to establish the production of crystallised fruit in Clermont-Ferrand. Certainly much of the fruit grown in the northern part of the Auvergne – peaches and apricots, apples and pears – is now used in this way. As for the taste of fresh fruit, you can judge for yourself by sampling the delicious wild strawberries and raspberries found along many of the paths to be described later.

Locally made liqueurs also benefited in the past from the special flavour of local fruit, but these are no longer produced. What has survived is an aperitif manufactured, on a moderate scale, in the town of Riom-es-Montagnes. The aperitif uses a liquid distilled from the root of the giant yellow gentian which grows prolifically in some parts of the Auvergne: you can see it particularly on Walk 26. It is sufficiently famous to have justified an exhibition each year from June to September at La Maison de la Gentiane et de la Flore in Riom, which makes a special feature of plants with medicinal or other uses.

Preparation Before You Go

The need to make extensive preparations before a trip abroad has largely disappeared in recent years as foreign travel has become more and more commonplace and restrictions have been relaxed. The only absolute essentials are a valid passport and sufficient money to see you through. Though this gives great freedom to the traveller, the vast majority of visitors will make travel and accommodation arrangements in good time, particularly if they are travelling at a busy time. August is undoubtedly the peak holiday period for the French, but since the six weeks from mid-July to the end of August, when things are at their busiest, correspond to school holidays in other countries, many people find they have little choice with regard to timing.

Do not let this put you off. Provided you have booked in advance, you will find that congestion is very rarely a problem. The Massif Central, because of its size and its low permanent population, can absorb huge numbers of visitors without giving the least impression of overcrowding. On the contrary, even in high summer you may well be puzzled by how few people you meet when walking, unless you happen to be near one of the more popular spots.

The key to this much-sought-after seclusion is a good map, and each of the walks described here notes the appropriate I.G.N. 1:25000 sheet. These are not cheap, in 1991 they cost about 46F, but they are quite accurate and do seem to be kept reasonably up to date. You can order them before you go, but they are so easily obtainable in all the popular walking areas that it may be better to buy a smaller scale map at home for your preliminary planning, waiting until you arrive to buy the more detailed maps.

Your preparations should include giving at least a little thought to the matter of insurance and health care. If booking through a travel agent, holiday insurance will be offered as a matter of course. In case of sudden illness, immediate medical treatment is provided under the European Community arrangements for visitors from the United Kingdom. But to get medical care you will need a Form E111 – the DHSS leaflet SA40, called 'Before You Go', will explain how to apply for one. Visitors from Australia, Canada and the USA will need to check the validity of their personal health insurance. No special vaccinations are necessary for France, for although there is now one available which develops immunity to rabies, it is not thought to be necessary unless there is an unusually high risk.

Health Hazards

The only real hazard at all likely to be met by the walker in the Auvergne is the heat. Unless you are used to it, you may well find that you have to set your sights rather lower than you would at home, doing shorter walks or less climbing. This has been borne in mind in planning the walks, but it is likely that you will be able to do more at the end of the holiday than at the beginning. The obvious precaution is to carry more liquid than normal, refreshment places – or even supplies of drinking water – being rarely found when you want them.

Sunstroke or severe sunburn evidently need to be guarded against, but these are not really a hazard unless you are foolish. Much the same applies to those well-publicised fears to which France seems particularly prone, snakes and rabid dogs. Certainly there is no shortage of aggressive dogs in the French countryside, but they do seem to be kept under control – behind high fences for the most part. But rabies is endemic, and anyone unfortunate enough to be bitten should seek immediate medical attention.

This is easier to than it sounds, since large villages as well as towns are likely to have a *pharmacie*, usually indicated by a large green cross, where, for a small fee, you can obtain first aid. Potentially more dangerous than a dog bite is the risk of a snake bite, if only because such an occurrence – unlikely though it may be – could take place a long way from a village, and immediate attention is again essential. Fortunately, every *pharmacie* sells an anti-snake bite serum, and it would be prudent to carry one in your first aid kit.

A much more probable hazard for the walker is the ubiquitous wire fence. Traditionally it is of barbed wire, closes off a path to stock, and is usually made to open easily. Increasingly, electric fences are being used. If properly installed, with a low voltage supply, it should be impossible to get a severe shock off them. Experience suggests, however, that, particularly in the more remote areas, cost-cutting has led to faulty or even illegal installations, so it pays to be wary.

A final point relates to the likelihood of your being alone in the event of an accident of any kind. The solitude of the Cantal mountains in particular, outside the holiday months of July and August, comes as a great surprise. It is hard to believe that weekend walking is so little practised, yet, during one superb ridge walk on a fine sunny Sunday in late May I met just one fellow walker, and that was my son, going the other way, and was more or less pre-arranged. Such loneliness is, of course, a consideration in the event of bad weather or accident. Mountain rescue facilities, if they exist, are certainly not well publicised. I came across just one mountain refuge, and although the *burons*, when they were in use, would have been occupied in the summer months at least, they are nowadays mainly in ruins.

The Country and the People

The Massif Central has been thought by some to be the least French part of France, largely because of its Celtic ancestry. There is certainly something in this argument; the Auvergne, at least, feels distinctly different from the rest of France, and some Celtic traditions have survived from the time when the Gallic hero, Vercingetorix, successfully held the ancient capital of Gregovia, near Clermont-Ferrand, against the Romans.

Much water has flowed under the bridges since then, but it is not surprising that the Auvergnats should have remained distinct from the French: Auvergne is a mountainous area, with difficult roads and a scattered population, which made it difficult to integrate the people with their more powerful neighbours. Moreover, mountain regions everywhere have tended to breed hardy and independent individuals with a disregard for convention and a suspicion of outsiders. Today that traditional wariness has all but disappeared, and you will find the people as friendly and forthcoming as anywhere in France.

As a consequence, you may find it difficult to put your finger on anything very distinctive about the Auvergnats nowadays, but their countryside is a different matter. The landscape does have a Celtic feel to it, especially the place-names which show similarities to those of Wales and Cornwall.

As to the appearance of the countryside, a wealth of stone walls and wayside crosses are reminiscent of the Celtic west of Britain while, even further back in time, pre-Celtic people are commemorated by their Megalithic tombs. The darkish-coloured stone of the volcanic region is said to give towns, villages, and particularly churches, a sombre appearance, but this is surely a matter of opinion. Certainly, the smallest and oldest churches are very dark inside, but this is due less to the colour of the stone than to the massive pillars and the tiny windows. The absence of high-level light from upper windows makes even the larger Romanesque churches seem rather dim, while the emphasis on pilgrimage, and the housing of the relics of the saints at the east end of the church, made it impracticable to provide a large east window. Perhaps the darkness was also intended to instil a proper sense of reverence.

It seems that religion has always played a large part in the lives of the people of the Auvergne, and this is certainly borne out by the bitterness of the conflict between Catholics and Protestants in the 16th and 17th centuries.

The St Bartholomew's Day massacre of Huguenots in Paris in 1572, which was followed by similar outbreaks in other parts of the country, precipitated a violent reaction in the Auvergne. Though it took some time for the Protestants to recover sufficiently to retaliate, the town of Issoire was taken and the Catholic population slaughtered in a hideous reprisal. Inevitably it was recaptured, by the Duc d'Anjou who killed thousands of Huguenots – not only in Issoire but in four hundred other villages, or so it is said, of the Auvergne. These terrible events were brought to an end in 1598, when the Edict of Nantes gave the Huguenots the right to practice their own form of religion. Violence remained in the air, however, for the aristocracy took the law into their own hands and imposed a tyrannical rule on the countryside which was only broken in 1632. Cardinal Richelieu, with the backing of the townspeople, then ordered the destruction of a great many baronial strongholds, particularly in the Auvergne, the ruinous condition of many of the châteaux dating from that time.

The French Revolution brought an end to the excesses of both church and aristocracy while permitting a new reign of terror no less dreadful than the old. To the peasants of the Auvergne, whose traditions were their life-blood, the destruction of the churches made no sense and they demonstrated in favour of God and the King. It was a futile gesture as it turned out, but it indicates the importance of both religion and continuity to country dwellers living in remote communities far from the ideals of Revolutionary France.

Perhaps a distinction should be drawn within Auvergne between those peasants cultivating the more fertile plains, accustomed to the unending toil associated with producing enough crops to pay the rent, and the relatively free life of the shepherds of the hills. The most important event of the shepherd's life was the *transhumance*, the annual movement of flocks and herds to the upland pastures in early summer, and their subsequent return in the autumn. The summer was spent free of interference from both landlord and priest, which encouraged dangerous free-thinking, but at the same time promoted religious and political tolerance. In practical terms the time was spent in caring for the animals, in milking and in cheese making, activities carried out at *burons*, the temporary shelters of the high pastures.

Many of these *burons* will be seen on the walks described, though few are now used in the ancient way and many are derelict. There is no longer the manpower available to permit such labour-intensive activities, except as a demonstration for visitors. Few hill pastures are now grazed by dairy herds because of the difficulty of milk collection, the main use now being for calf-rearing, in conjunction with the valley farms, new roads having been cut to allow the uplands to be visited daily with motor transport.

For these and other reasons, the hill farmer is now much more likely to be using part of his land for tourist activities, camping, caravanning, swimming, and fishing, or providing overnight or holiday accommodation. There is no reluctance to provide facilities for tourists, for the people of the Auvergne are only too well aware of their importance to the local economy, but, thankfully, the more tawdry side of tourism is usually kept well in the background, while hospitality is brought to the fore. In every town, and many of the villages, you will find a Tourist Office with literature relating to the district. There will be someone there willing to help you with problems, and increasingly they speak English.

While walking in the countryside, everyone you meet, locals and visitors alike, will pass the time of day. *Bonjour* is the usual greeting, the formality of it coming as something of a surprise. Do not construe this formality as lack of warmth. If you ask *pouvez vous m'aider?* (can you help me?) you will invariably meet with a sympathetic response, and they will finish by wishing you *bonne route*. Since foreign tourists are so rare they will naturally assume at first that you are also French, and in the case of other walkers they may well be asking you for help rather than the other way round. In that case it will be of enormous benefit to have at least a few words of French. Local farmers on the other hand, if you reveal your nationality, will want to know all about you – but from natural curiosity rather than suspicion. If you have any queries about the route, they will be only too happy to help you, and, provided you show due consideration, you are most unlikely to meet any hostility whether you are following the correct line of the path or not.

Further Information

In case of serious accident, telephone 17 for the police or 18 for the fire service. They will inform the ambulance service as it has no national call-out number, though the number of the local service should be displayed in every public telephone box.

There is no regular system of registration for visitors entering the country. Hotels do not even ask to see your passport, providing you have booked in advance, but you may be asked to produce it in other circumstances. Remember that motoring offences can carry heavy on-the-spot fines, payable in cash. The minimum fine for speeding is 600F, and that for exceeding the drink-driving level is 1200F. Remember that France has random breath tests.

Postage stamps are sold at Post Offices, but also at newsagents and other shops where postcards are sold. The postal rates change from time to time, so you will have to enquire. Public telephones usually take 5F, 2F, and 1F coins, and sometimes smaller denominations. To ring the U.K. you dial 19 – 44, to ring Australia it is 19 – 61, for Canada and the USA dial 19 – 1. Remember to omit the initial zero of the area code.

Organised events in the Auvergne vary from place to place, some areas taking them very seriously, while other ignore them completely. In the Sancy-Artense region, the northern half of the Auvergne, the published programme for August usually shows events on every day, though these will be scattered over the whole region.

The nature of the events will be extremely varied, most being loosely classed as cultural – from rock concerts to chamber music – and the remainder featuring sporting events. Lectures, films, and demonstrations are also conspicuous, though the many permanent exhibitions and museums will not be included in the list. There are good folk museums at Saint-Flour and Aurillac; there is also a geological museum at Aurillac, a natural history museum at Murat, and a museum featuring the history of ski-ing at Besse. In addition, there is a multitude of demonstrations to be seen at various locations, featuring aspects of life in the Auvergne. There are also guided tours of the older towns, and special interest guided walks relating to the botany or the wildlife of particular areas. To get much out of these last events you will need to be reasonably proficient in the French language.

Detailed information on all events can be obtained from local tourist information offices, which exist in all the larger villages, though they function only in the holiday season and their opening hours may be limited. The larger regional offices are open all the year. The principal offices are:

For the northern Auvergne:
      Comité Departement de Tourisme,
      17 Place Delille,
      63038 Clermont-Ferrand

For Cantal:
      Maison du Tourisme,
      22 Rue Guy de Veyre,
      BP 8 – 15018 Aurillac

For Saint-Flour:
      Bureau de Tourisme,
      2 Place d'Armes,
      15100 Saint-Flour

Information relating particularly to the *Parc des Volcans* can be obtained from:

> Centre d'Information Permanent,
> Regional Parc des Volcans
> 10 Rue du President Delzons,
> Aurillac

The Organisation of the Walks

With both accessibility and the choice of the best possible walking routes in the locality in mind, eight different centres have been chosen in Auvergne, with walks beginning at that centre or a short distance away. It will be clear that, because the centres themselves are conveniently linked by either public or private transport, a much larger group of walks is available from each centre than is described under that heading alone. Preceding each group of walks is a short introduction to the town or village which forms the centre, noting not only its attractions but also its facilities and, particularly, its range of accommodation.

The first group of centres – four in all – is distributed around the Cantal massif, allowing exploration from several different angles. The first is Murat, an old town, where a number of interesting buildings have survived. Not far from Murat is another ancient town, Saint-Flour, built on a hill-top, though with a medieval suburb close to the river bridge at the foot of a cliff. The walks from here have rather more of a lowland character than those of Murat. If, instead, you travel in the other direction, tunnelling under the mountains of Cantal, either by road or rail, you come to the beautiful valley of the Cère where two more centres – those of Vic-sur-Cère and Thiézac – give access to two further groups of walks of a distinctly more mountainous character.

In the northern part of the Auvergne there are two separate and distinct types of landscape. Les Monts Dore is a mountain group centred on the Puy de Sancy, the heavily glaciated remnant of a huge volcano some sixty million years old. The relatively modern spa towns of Le Mont-Dore and La Bourboule, lying in the valley of the infant Dordogne, are both good walking centres – with the latter perhaps having the edge because of the greater variety available. Here, the walks are described as starting La Bourboule, though since the towns are only a short distance apart, they can be accessed equally well from either. On the other side of Les Monts Dore lie the small towns of Saint-Nectaire, another spa, and Besse-en-Chandesse. Though there are no rail links to these centres, they can be reached quite easily by road from Clermont Ferrand. Perhaps the hardest walk is the book, Walk 21, features the ascent of Puy de Sancy from Monneau, which is midway between Saint-Nectaire and La Bourboule and accessible from either.

Finally, we come to the most unusual landscape to be found in the Auvergne, that of the Chaîne des Puys, a chain consisting of 112 relic volcanoes according to one estimate. The last eruptions were sufficiently recent for the peaks to be seen as individual cones of volcanic ash, some of them cratered, the craters, in many instances, occupied by beautiful lakes. Whilst this area provides splendid walking, accommodation is scarce; the walks therefore necessitate some travelling from those places offering the necessary facilities. Besse-en-Chandesse is conveniently placed for the southern volcanoes, and Orcival is not too far from those to the north.

Some comment is necessary regarding the character of the walking. The highest summit reached is Puy de Sancy which, at 1,885m, is also the highest peak of the Massif Central. The actual height to be climbed on any walk hardly exceeds 700m however, and the gradients are not too steep. The walks cover a range of terrain from easy grass slopes to steep rocky crags.

THE WALKS

Murat

Murat is situated at an important junction of routes, where the road, and railway, running roughly east-west along the Alagnon valley is crossed by the road from Saint-Flour towards Mauriac. The town lies 50 kilometres from Aurillac and 110 kilometres from Clermont-Ferrand. As the natural focus of the upland farming region of eastern Cantal, it became a flourishing cattle market and a distribution centre for Cantal cheese. The cheeses were formerly made by hand at the *burons* of the high plateaux, between May and September when the flocks and herds grazed the upland pastures. Modern changes in the pattern of hill farming have caused this practice to be virtually abandoned, and Murat has become the manufacturing centre for factory-made cheese, though the townsfolk are also heavily engaged in forestry.

During the Middle Ages Murat was a fortified town with no less than seven gates. Surprisingly, it was situated neither at the river crossing, nor at one of the local hilltop sites which had been occupied in prehistoric times, but below the basalt crag of Bonnevie. This position makes sense only if there was protection from a fortress sited on the rock, and in fact the Vicomtes of Murat held a château, consisting of a strong keep surrounded by three concentric defensive walls, on top of the crag. The fortress was demolished in 1633, the site now being occupied by a massive statue of the Virgin erected in 1878. The statue is the best point from which to appreciate the layout of the town below.

Though subject to the regular fires which seriously damaged all congested medieval towns. Murat has retained a number of houses, often the homes of notable families, dating from the late Middle Ages onwards. By that time Murat had evidently outgrown its defensive walls: for the fine consular house of the late 15th century lay outside. Many of the ancient buildings are marked by plaques, and are readily found by visitors who walk the narrow streets. To derive the maximum from a walk ask for a town plan at the Hôtel de Ville. The church of Notre Dame des Oliviers takes its name from a statue of the Virgin which, according to legend, was brought here from the Holy Land. The statue survived a fire that necessitated the rebuilding of the church in 1494, only to be stolen in 1983: the church now contains only a modern copy. Some of the precious objects removed from St Anthony's chapel (see

Woolly Thistle

Walk 1) when it was abandoned are to be found here. One of the ancient administrative buildings of the town, just off the main square, is now a museum of natural history.

The town centre has no hotels, for they are all sensibly situated near the railway station. On the Avenue du Dr. Mallet are to be found Les Messagèries and Aux Globe-Trotteurs, both two star. Nearby, on the Rue du Faubourg, are the Central Hôtel and the Hôtel du Stade. Nearly all these hotels have restaurants, but there are further places to eat in the old town, including the Auberge de Maitre Paul in the Place du Planol and the Restaurant de la Paix in the Rue St Martin. There is just one camp site, the Camping Municipal with a 2-star rating, situated outside the town on the banks of the Alagnon.

Walk 1   Chastel-sur-Murat

Map:	IGN 1:25000 2435 Est, Murat et Plomb du Cantal
Time:	$2^1/_2$ hours walking
Grade:	Easy, apart from two short climbs
Ascent:	400 metres including options

A short and easy walk, but with two optional climbs to superb viewpoints.

The Walk

Start from the Hôtel de Ville of Murat, in the town square.

The Hôtel de Ville houses the Tourist Office and if, on leaving the front door, you follow the building round to your right, then take the first turning to the left, you will find yourself in the Rue du Bon Secours. Go straight up the street, past numerous old buildings (some just off this street), and round the back of the church, continuing up the hill around several bends along the Rue de Lavergnes. Emerging on to the main road at the top, go straight across, following a path signposted to the Rocher de Bonnevie, which is the basalt cliff overhanging the town. After a short distance, and immediately before reaching the main road again, the track turns left and climbs between old drystone walls of dark-coloured basalt.

The way is known as the Chemin des Croix, and you pass no less than fourteen crucifixes on your way up to the huge, and rather too obvious, white statue of the Virgin. It was erected in 1878, on the site previously occupied by a château, though that had been pulled down in 1633 on the orders of Richelieu. The view of the town below is of the kind normally seen only in aerial photographs, the limits of the medieval town being clearly visible. South-east lies the rock of Bredons, featured in Walk 2, and easily within view looking north-west is your next destination, the great crag above Chastel-sur-Murat.

Descend by the same route, but this time emerging on to the main road and turning right, then left after 200 metres along the D680. You soon arrive at the hamlet of l'Heritier and turn off right up a stony track after passing an

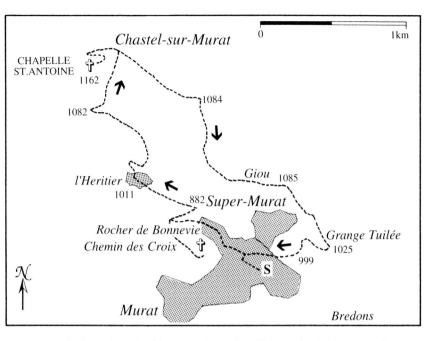

CHAPELLE ST.ANTOINE
1162
1082
Chastel-sur-Murat
0   1km
1084
l'Heritier
1011
Giou   1085
882 Super-Murat
Rocher de Bonnevie
Chemin des Croix
Grange Tuilée
1025
999
S
N
Murat
Bredons

immensely long farm building on the right. The track climbs up under a
massively-built wall, then doubles back across pasture land, heading directly
for the crag of Chastel-sur-Murat. This is a favourite haunt of birds of prey,
and you will be unfortunate not to see both buzzards and red kites in some
numbers. The fields here, though quite large, have been terraced (with
immense labour) towards the south. The work could only have been justified
by the need to plough for the growing of cereal crops, which are no longer
grown here. This suggestion seems to be confirmed by the huge barns of the
ruined farm you pass on your right, far larger than would be needed for the hay
crop alone.

After passing the ruins, the path swings right, becoming a terraced
quarrymen's track under the basalt pillars of the cliff. Entering the village,
turn left along a footpath directly opposite the church door, and climb the zig-
zag path to the Chapelle St Antoine, passing the socketed base of a former
cross on the way. Though the church is now disused – apart, perhaps, from
the belfry, reached by an external staircase – the stripped interior has
regained some of its authentic medieval austerity. There is a strong feeling of
unity with the rock on which it was built, strengthened by the way it is set
into the ground, making it necessary to descend a flight of steps into the nave
of the tiny cruciform church. As a viewpoint the rock, being higher than the

The old town centre of Murat

Rocher de Bonnevie, gives a better view westwards, where the sharp peak of Puy Griou is particularly prominent.

Return to the village and take the track to the south of the church, heading south-east. After half a kilometre or so it is necessary to look carefully for a yellow-waymarked stone on the right, at the point where a track comes in from the left. Turn right across the wire fence and along the field edge with a ditch on your left. At the top of the field, rather than climbing the lynchet bank into the next field, turn slightly left into a grassy lane continuing in the same direction. It is bounded by stone walls and is perfectly clear, though not much used. Follow it forward to pass under the edge of a pine wood. The landscape here is remarkable, not only for the tiny size of the lyncheted fields – indicating the need to use every scrap of cultivable land – but also for the great height of the boundary lynchets.

They were necessary partly to create fields level enough to plough, on this very steep slope, but also, one suspects, to provide a tip for the enormous number of stones and boulders which had to be cleared from the hillside before a plough could be driven through the earth. It all suggests a large population struggling to make a living by farming pitifully inadequate land at some time long since gone, but probably in the early Middle Ages, before the Black Death cut back the population and made it unnecessary to farm

St Anthony's Chapel

marginal land. Eventually, at Giou, the terraced track becomes a proper road, which you leave at the first of the new houses in favour of the green track passing to the left of them. This shortly rejoins the road: turn left and follow it down to Grange Tuilée. Cross the D39 here, and follow the road which swings right and takes you down into the old town of Murat, where you emerge behind the church of Notre Dame des Oliviers.

Walk 2   Bredons and Les Cunes

Map:	IGN 1:25000 2435 Est, Murat et Plomb du Cantal
Time:	4 hours walking
Grade:	Easy, apart from two fairly steep climbs
Ascent:	360 metres

Mostly on level tracks, but with a short climb to Bredons, and a steeper, longer, climb to Les Cunes.

The Walk

Start from the Hotel de Ville of Murat, in the town square.

Take the D926, the main road out of the town, going south-east towards Saint-Flour for nearly a kilometre to the bridge over the Alagnon river and, after crossing, turn right up a waymarked path climbing towards the church of Bredons, visible above. The direction is misleading, however, for the path, instead of taking you to the church, makes for the edge of the village, where you turn left along the road to find the church at the top of a cliff.

The village, in spite of much recent rebuilding, and despite the 19th century dates on some door lintels recalling the previous phase of reconstruction, appears ancient. Stone crosses on many of the roofs add to this impression, as do the farmhouses with huge attached barns which are typical of the district. The main reason though, comes from the hilltop situation and the clear fact that it is still a cul-de-sac as far as vehicles are concerned. The basaltic crag on which the village is built would have made it easy to defend, but the origins of the settlement seem to be lost in antiquity. It is known that there was a monastery here in 1060, and the predominance of Bredons, even over Murat, as the parochial centre for the surrounding district makes it likely that it was an important early Christian site.

Its name, too, suggests a Celtic ancestry, so it is not surprising to find at least two examples of stone-carved 'Celtic heads' in the village. One of them looks relatively modern and is built into a barn wall, and suggests nothing more than an attempt to revive an old tradition, but a much older one is built

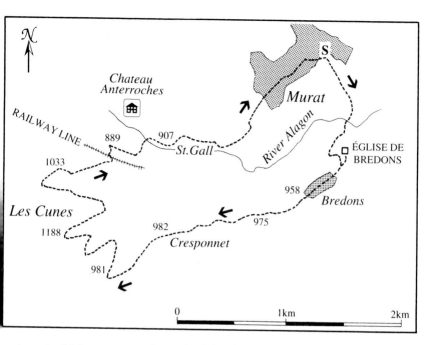

into the 11th century south porch of the church. However, this church was pulled down at the time of the Revolution, and was only rebuilt at the beginning of this century, so it may have been inserted at that time.

When you are ready to leave this fascinating place, head straight down the village street, past the cross, to reach the circular village fountain at the bottom. Continue forward here on a waymarked track which keeps just below the crest of the ridge. This is an easy, level, walk, with good views to the north, and passes above the farmhouse at Cresponnet, and just below the conifer plantations, before emerging on the D39 just below Grange de Magne. Red Kites seem to be active in some numbers here in early summer, perhaps attracted by rodents made homeless by haymaking.

Turn right on reaching the road, but after descending no more than 100 metres, turn left immediately after crossing the bridge. At the first fork, soon after, turn left again and start to climb up a steep stony track, whose gradient, fortunately, eases the higher you go. The track makes several abrupt turns, but the only place where it is possible to go wrong is on a section heading north-east, when Bredons is visible nearly ahead, and where you have to turn back sharply left along a less-obvious track than the one you were following. Fortunately, a crossed waymark indicates clearly enough that the track ahead is not the correct way. After making the turn the track is obstructed in one

The fountain at Bredons

or two places by fallen trees, though none of them will cause any difficulty. Indeed, at one point a pair of trees have fallen outwards, most considerately, leaving a clear path between their respective roots.

Eventually, the track levels out on the plateau of Les Cunes, and even starts to descend, leading north through thin woodland along the top of the crags that had appeared so high and so distant from below. The path emerges on to a bulldozed track. Turn right along the track following it as it descends, curving round the northern nose of the ridge, towards the west. Eventually it makes a sharp turn to the north, as clearly indicated by yellow waymarks, and descends to a metalled road. Turn right here, but after only 50 metres turn left, down a path which initially runs parallel to the road but then descends more steeply, through woodland, before crossing the railway line.

The green lane continues for a further 200 metres, then joins another, parallel to the valley, along which you turn right. Follow the track as it twists, first left, then right after crossing a stream (the Alagnon again) by a plank bridge, where the Chateau of Anterroches is visible on the hillside ahead. Finally, you arrive on the main road (the N122) at St Gall and turn right along it. You can follow it all the way into Murat but, to avoid its busy traffic, turn right after passing the cemetery and join the minor road from Albepierre-Bredons, which returns you to the main road much nearer the town.

Walk 3   Les Issarts

Map:	IGN 1:25000 2435 Est, Murat et Plomb du Cantal
Time:	4 hours walking
Grade:	Easy, unless the chapel is visited
Ascent:	200 metres (plus 230 metres to the chapel)

An easy walk throughout, on good paths with a limited amount of climbing on gentle gradients.

The Walk

Start from the church of Notre Dame des Oliviers in Murat.

Leave the town by taking the Rue Marchadiat, which starts at the back of the church and climbs steadily in an easterly direction. As you climb, there are ample opportunities to turn and view the basaltic columns which make up the mass of the Rocher de Bonnevie, and to appreciate the amphitheatrical siting of the town below it. At the only road junction turn right, to arrive on the D39 at the hamlet of Ezoldebeau. Go straight across, climbing north-west, with the new houses of Super-Murat on your left. When you reach the first new houses on your right, leave the road in favour of the green track, also to the right, which passes behind them. After 200 metres or so you emerge on to the road again at the point where the metalled surface finishes: continue forward along the farm track – ignoring another track turning back on the right – to reach the farm of Giou, which is reached by passing between massive stone walls.

At Giou, carry on in the same direction, with the farm on your right, along a waymarked green terrace which eventually passes beneath a conifer plantation and then swings northwards. Along the whole of this terraced section there are expansive views, westward towards the mountains of Cantal and northward towards the chapel of St Anthony on its rock. The route is not always well-trodden, but the way ahead is clear, being bounded by stone walls. As the path descends, it begins to get rather overgrown, and it may be better to move into the field on your left, an easy alternative since there is no

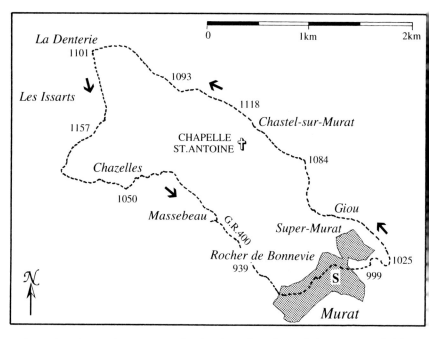

boundary fence. You soon reach a hard track and turn left, past remarkably tall, spire-like ash trees, to arrive at the village of Chastel-sur-Murat.

You can climb to St Anthony's chapel by taking the footpath that starts opposite the church door, the reward being a vast panorama, not only of the Cantal mountains, but of the great plateaux of volcanic lava. Areas such as the Limon plateau, a few miles to the north-west, were too high and exposed for year-round occupation. They were therefore used as seasonal pastures, the flocks and herds being taken up at the great stock movement, known as the *transhumance*, in early summer.

If you have already visited the chapel you may prefer to continue north-westerly along the D139, ignoring a right turn to Lapsou to reach the junction with the D680. Cross the main road at 45 degrees and go down a grassy terrace, so well-engineered that it must have been part of the former highway, to emerge past a diminutive disused chapel in the village of La Denterie.

Turn left on reaching the road (D139) and follow it through the village. At the stream crossing beyond, turn left, over the lower of the two bridges, and climb up the hill on a grassy track. It is very evident around here, where birds of prey are constantly in view, that the small birds heard twittering in the tree tops prefer to stay under the canopy of leaves, a wise precaution. Half way up the hill, ignore the left turn and continue in a straight line, through

Near Chastel-sur-Murat

the woods, to emerge on the road again at the top. Turn left, to reach, in a few metres, the top of the hill. Here another vast panorama unfolds, from Plomb du Cantal in the south-west, round by way of Puy Griou to Puy Mary lying almost due west. Ignore the track turning right at the top, serving the moorland enclosures called Les Issarts. The name is taken from the Old French *essarter*, meaning to clear wasteland. Instead, make a right turn as the road starts to descend, going along a stony track that heads south-west.

This is yet another old road, taking a straighter line than the modern one. After 100 metres you leave the track by turning half-left, along a wire fence, to rejoin the road further down. In some seasons, when the undergrowth is luxuriant, it may be better to miss out this section and simply walk down the road. In either case you arrive at a crossways, where the metalled road turns right. Continue straight ahead on a green track between high hedges. The track leads gently down to Chazelles, where you turn right in front of the house, across the middle of a meadow, taking a faint path that follows the line of the overhead cables.

The way becomes clearer as you descend, though the going is rather wet underfoot in some places, and is clearly waymarked with red and white stripes at strategic points. In addition, the road you are making for, which follows the valley floor, is clearly in view ahead. Join the road where it ends, and turn

Chazelles

right along it (south-east) as far as the Château of Massebeau. Turn right, then immediately left, in front of the château, and follow the track through a conifer plantation to emerge on the Murat by-pass. Turn right, downhill, and go left after a few metres along a grassy track, to enter the modern part of the town by the side of a supermarket. Turn left here for the old town.

Vic-Sur-Cère

The town of Vic-sur-Cère has been a spa since Roman times, though the medicinal springs and, perhaps, the Roman settlement seem to have been a little way from the medieval town. The latter grew up in the shadow of the feudal château, set on a crag above the church at a site now known as Le Castel Viel, visited at the end of the first walk. Vic consists of two quite distinct parts: the old town, which received a boost in the 17th century following a visit from Anne of Austria, wife of Louis XIII; and a newer town which resulted from an expansion of the spa facilities in the 19th century.

The old town still retains some early buildings, the oldest, dating from the 15th century, being called the Maison des Princes de Monaco. The Princes were granted a large estate locally by Louis XIII and, it is believed, administered it from here right up to the time of the French Revolution, though the house itself must have been quite old when they acquired it. Many of Vic's ancient houses have roofs constructed of heavy stone fish-scale slates known as 'lauzes' or 'lozes'. The name is associated with Mont Lozere, a high point towards the southern margin of the Massif Central, where there were slate quarries.

The town sets out to attract visitors by providing a wide range of facilities, and has a good selection of hotels and restaurants, one group of which is situated in the old town and the other across the river, near the railway station and the spa. Hotels on the main street of the old town – or just off it – include the two largest, the Beauséjour and the Vialette, both of which are two star; two medium-sized one star establishments, Le Relais and La Terrasse; and the Central (a Hôtel Préfecture). The restaurant Paris-Auvergne also has a few rooms.

Near the station you will find the Bel Horizon, the Grand Hôtel des Sources, and the Touring-Hôtel, with the Hôtel des Bains not far away. All of these are two star, the Saint Joseph being a one star. Other hotels and restaurants can be found at the ends of the town and in nearby villages. The Auberge des Trois Chemins at Salvanhac, for example, has a restaurant specialising in local dishes, and 6 kilometres away, up at the Col de Curebourse, the Auberge des Monts offers a similar cuisine. Other accommodation available includes the three star Camping Municipal, by the river and close to the town. About 2 kilometres away is La Pommeraie, a four star camp site with its own swimming pool, restaurant and bar.

Walk 4　Grotte des Anglais & La Garde

Map:	IGN 1:25000 2436 Ouest. Vic-sur-Cère
Time:	2$^1/_2$ hours walking
Grade:	Moderate
Ascent:	400 metres

Though only a short route, the path is a little difficult to find in places.

The Walk

Start from the Place de l'Eglise, Vic-sur-Cère.

Follow the street north-eastwards to join the main road, and walk along it towards Thiézac and Murat. After under a kilometre, fork right at the sign to La Prade, then take the upper of the two metalled roads at a barn that is complemented by an Auvergne-style dovecote. Follow the road, originally constructed by Napoleon's army some 200 years ago as part of the Route Imperiale, to Fournols. At Fournols, take the track signposted to the Cascade de Fournols, which is pretty but unspectacular. There are reputed to be three superimposed bridges here: a Roman one, surmounted by a Napoleonic bridge, with a modern one on top, but the distinction needs the eye of faith. It is possible to follow the Imperial route further, but it becomes progressively more overgrown, so return to Fournols and take the right turn up the hill to the main road, with the cliff, your next objective, towering above.

Turn right along the main road, then, after 100 metres, take the second path on the left, signposted to the Grotte des Anglais. The path climbs steeply for a while: when it starts to level out, take the footpath doubling back on the left, as indicated by red waymarks. This traverses a steep hillside to reach the large cave (*grotte*) in the cliff face, which was the reputed hideout of mercenaries fighting for the English during the Hundred Years War. It is now necessary to retrace your steps to the main path, turning left on reaching it and following red waymarks which have now become circles rather than bars. The path is easy until it turns sharply to the left at a waymark and climbs a steep hillside. The gradient eases, then steepens again and, just when you are beginning to think you have lost the path (it is very faint at this point),

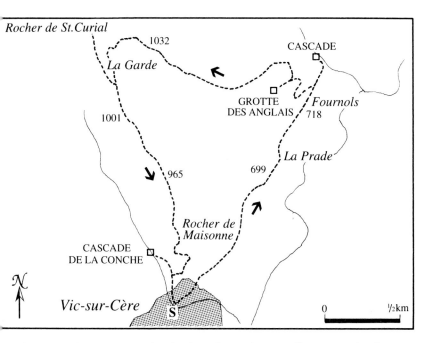

the waymarks re-appear. They lead you forward to a small outcrop of rocks on a plateau, surrounded by foxgloves and giant yellow gentians. Turn left, descend for a few paces, then follow the contours to pick up the waymarks again in thin oak woodland.

A view of the surrounding hills starts to open up from some of the more open clearings, and you soon arrive at a wire fence forming the boundary between woodland and pasture. Cross the fence and follow it to the right for 200 metres, leaving it by turning left through the middle of a small copse. The waymarks show the line, but since the marks tend to be on the opposite side of the tree-trunks to the way you are going, it is as well, on emerging from the copse, to make for the left hand side of the small hill ahead. On rounding it, you should see the farm of La Garde ahead of you. Instead of making straight for it keep slightly to the right, where you will pick up the line of an old, deeply-worn, track.

The old track crosses a bracken-covered heath, with occasional birches, field roses, and dog roses, and seems to be home to a whole host of jays. One of the surprises is the almost total absence of crows and rooks, the usual scavengers, and their replacement by kites, magpies, and jays. The track itself is somewhat overgrown until you pass the ruins of a *buron* on the right, after which it becomes much easier. The path goes around the head of the valley

The Rocher de St Curial

to the farm of La Garde. Cross the fence and go behind the house, descending again immediately to reach a gate by the barn, where the farm road begins.

There is the site of an ancient hermitage in the cliff behind the house, but it is not particularly easy to find from this point. It is better to follow the farm road downhill for 200 metres, where you will find a sign indicating the way, right, to the cliff, which is known as the Rocher de St Curial. After exploring the area and savouring the views towards l'Elancèze, visited by a later walk, return to the farm road and follow it downhill for over half a kilometre (from la Garde) to a point where it swings to the right. There is normally a fence across the road here. Leave the road immediately before the fence and cross the stile to the left, as indicated by the signpost to Maisonne. Pass through the hedge and follow the obvious path downhill, taking the left-hand fork when the path divides. Though this new path is narrow, it is well-trodden and takes you through the woodland to a ridge surmounted by the crags known as the Rocher de Maisonne. From the bench by the Cross there is a spectacular view of Vic, below, and the Cère valley. Follow the path as it descends steeply through woods, stepping aside to see the rock of Le Castel Viel, site of the former feudal stronghold which dominated the town. Finally, there is an opportunity to visit a small waterfall, the Cascade de la Conche, before arriving at the rear of the parish church in the old part of Vic.

Walk 5   Pas de Cère & Thiézac

Maps:	IGN 1:25000 2436 Ouest, Vic-sur-Cère; & 2435 Ouest, Thiézac
Time:	4 hours walking
Grade:	Easy
Ascent:	200 metres

Easy walking throughout, with the impressive gorge of Pas de Cère as the high point.

The Walk

Start from the Place de l'Eglise, Vic-sur-Cère.

From the parish church walk eastwards along the Rue Bertrand, then cross the main street to leave the town by way of the Avenue Murat Sistrières. Continue straight ahead where this turns right, passing the cemetery and the municipal camp site, and walk along the road beside the river. After crossing the bridge, take the left fork, signposted to Salvanhac-Bas. Go through the village, leaving the road where a track forks off left at a sign to Pas de Cère. Follow the track until, just before reaching a gate across the way, you turn right at another sign along a footpath crossing meadows.

On reaching the river, cross the footbridge to the right, over a former mill race, and walk along the river bank. Above and to the right can be seen the restored manor house of Tremoulet, which will be seen at close quarters later on. The Pas de Cère, when it eventually appears, astonishes by its size, being a tremendously deep gorge – created at a great step in the valley floor – through which the river drops in a series of small waterfalls. Before crossing the footbridge you will see that an artificial watercourse has been constructed at some time, and later filled in, presumably tapping the river at a natural weir to drive a water mill at Salvanhac.

Cross the bridge and turn right, to find, perhaps to your surprise, that the path passes through the jaws of the gorge. You follow the stream, with the path sometimes high above the river and sometimes level with it, but there seems to be no point from which you can seen the gorge in its entirety. The

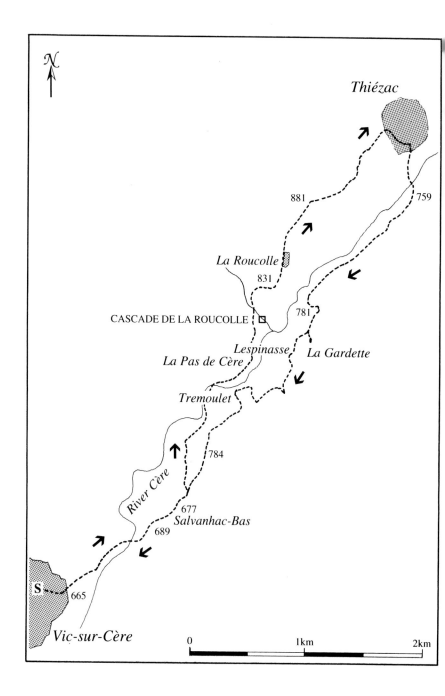

N

Thiézac

881

759

La Roucolle

831

CASCADE DE LA ROUCOLLE

781

Lespinasse

La Pas de Cère

La Gardette

Tremoulet

784

River Cère

677

689

Salvanhac-Bas

S

665

Vic-sur-Cère

0   1km   2km

stream has, incidentally, been dammed upstream of the gorge in times past to create a millpool, but the dam has been broken by the force of the water. These attempts at exploitation for rural industry are made to seem very puny, compared to the vast scale of the landscape changes wrought by nature. Just before emerging on to a road, turn right to the viewpoint overlooking the confluence of the Cère and its tributary from the village of Lasmolineries, from which point another waterfall, the Cascade de la Roucolle, is visible. Once on the main road, turn right, cross the river, and turn left, following the old road up to La Roucolle. Follow the road right through the hamlet, turning to the right when you join the D59 at the top. Fork right immediately afterwards, but 100 metres after passing a house on the left, go straight ahead when the road swings right, along the track signposted to Cap de la Garde. This will take you directly to the main road, just outside the village of Thiézac.

Turn left along the main road through the village, and at its centre turn right, down the road leading to the bridge over the Cère. After crossing, turn right again, past the fish farm. Soon the lane becomes a green track with yellow waymarks: follow these until you become aware that, without your climbing, the river you have been following is now far below you, having begun its descent of the Pas de Cère. The appearance of an embankment reinforced by brick arches on your left now alerts you to the presence of the railway above, and you turn left shortly afterwards, going under the railway line.

The path now climbs to cross a small stream, then doubles back and rounds a promontory. Soon you emerge on the road below La Gardette, at a point where there is an extensive view northwards towards the valley containing the village of Lasmolineries, and the green hills above it. Turn right, down the road, then left immediately before the farm of Lespinasse. The road follows the edge of the woods above the railway, crossing it at the entrance to a short tunnel. The road now reaches the well-restored and magnificently-sited manor house of Tremoulet, complete with its dovecote. In France, as elsewhere, only the Lord of the Manor was allowed to keep and eat the pigeons which devastated his tenant's crops. Turn left at the entrance to the farm and cross the railway twice more to reach Salvanhac-Bas, where you rejoin the outward route for a return walk to Vic.

Walk 6   Pas de la Mougudo & the Roman road

Maps:	IGN 1:25000 2436 Ouest, Vic-sur-Cère; & 2435 Ouest, Thiézac
Time:	6 hours walking
Grade:	Moderate but lengthy
Ascent:	700 metres

The Plomb du Cantal, as the highest mountain in the vicinity, is a natural objective for walkers, but is not, to be honest, a very attractive climb. Some of the views it offers can be sampled by walking the long ridge leading towards it, a ridge taken by a Roman road.

The Walk

Start at the Place de l'Eglise, Vic-sur-Cère.

The walk starts from the parish church, heading east along the Rue Bertrand. Cross the main street in to the Avenue Murat Sistrieres and go straight ahead where that road turns right, so as to follow the road towards Salvanhac. After crossing the bridge, take the right fork for Salvanhac-Haut. At the centre of the village turn left, then right under the railway arch. Now turn left up a stony track signposted to the Pas de la Mougudo and waymarked in yellow. A field wall to the left, an orchard in fact, is attractively planted with roses, irises, and lilies, and the path is roughly paved as it climbs straight up the hill before making a right turn along the hillside. From here there are fine views down to Vic.

Soon the path starts climbing again, but it is well-shaded by oak, ash, beech and chestnut as it zig-zags up past a ruined cottage with the delightful name of Chante-Coucou. At the nearby barn turn right, ignoring the confusing waymark, and follow the track to arrive at the base of a cliff, the Pas de la Mougudo. Continue forward, crossing a stream course and climbing the steep hillside up the well-graded path, to emerge from the woods on to the road where it crosses a bracken-covered hillside. Turn right and enjoy the extensive views, up the Cère valley to Puy Griou, and down towards Aurillac. After little more than a kilometre of this road, turn left up a broad track

44

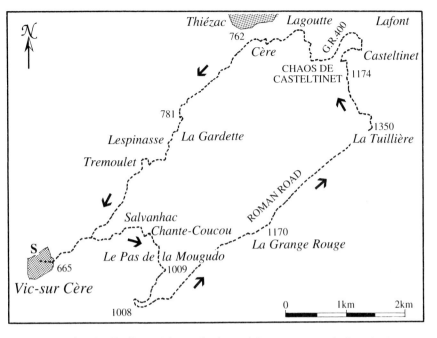

signposted to La Tuillière. This is the line of the Roman road, though there is no sign now of Roman construction. It is a fine ridge, and allows you to climb without appreciable effort to a height where the air is more bracing, the views more extensive, and the vegetation more alpine. You will be accompanied by buzzards, kites, and ravens, but provided you avoid weekends and public holidays, when La Tuillière becomes a popular venue for four-wheel drive motorists, you are likely to have it very much to yourself. Once past La Grange Rouge, you can avoid some of the bends of the modern track by taking the older, straighter, and steeper, line marked by a hollow way. Eventually, you top a small rise and drop down to the *buron* of La Tuillière, a good place for a break, since it offers refreshments and is usually open.

On leaving the *buron*, the path down to Thiézac, which is a Grande Randonnée and should be waymarked with red and white bars, is by no means obvious. But if you turn left along the walled track immediately below the house, then turn half-right when the right-hand wall starts to swing away, you should pick up a clear track descending the hillside to your left. It zig-zags down fairly steeply, and on emerging from a belt of woodland crosses a newly-bulldozed track at 45 degrees. Continue forward on the same line to cross a fence into an open pasture. Cross a second fence to pass between a craggy knoll on your right and a smoothly-rounded knoll on your left. The path now swings left around a promontory, with Thiézac coming into view below, then drops down on to a farm road.

Cross the road, taking the path directly opposite, which cuts off the corner and brings you out on to the road again near the farm of Casteltinet. At the second hairpin bend below the farm, where the road doubles back right, go straight ahead, maintaining almost the same level, to reach a waymarked post by a wire fence. Cross the fence, climb a few feet, contour under the cliff, then follow the now much-improved path which descends gently below the cliff. This path can be rather slippery under some conditions and if, after trying it, you feel it is not for you, go back to the road and descend to Lagoutte by way of Lafont. If you are staying with the path, watch for the frequent red, white, and yellow waymarks, turning left, as directed, back up the hill at one point, to pass the massive fallen boulders known as the Chaos de Casteltinet at the foot of the cliff. The path keeps to the boundary between woodland and pasture where possible and, after passing through a clearing, descends to join the road beside the railway.

Go under the bridge and through the village of Lagoutte, turning right 200 metres below the village to follow the old road down. Ignore the right turn by the thatched barn, but join the road at the next junction, at the hamlet of Cère. Turn right here and follow the road between the tennis courts and the sports field to the bridge below Thiézac, continuing straight ahead past the fish farm. The lane becomes a green track, with yellow waymarks, which you follow to reach a left turn under the railway line. The path then climbs for a short distance, crosses a stream, and doubles back around a promontory. Emerging on the road below La Gardette, turn right, then left immediately before the farm of Lespinasse. Cross the railway again, at the entrance to a tunnel, to reach Tremoulet. Turn left there and cross the railway twice more before arriving at Salvanhac-Bas. Go straight through the village to rejoin the outward route which returns you to Vic.

Thiézac

This village of only 740 inhabitants lies on a steep, south-east facing, hillside on the road from Murat to Vic-sur-Cère. It seems to consist of just two streets, the main road and a parallel road a little higher up the hill. The architecture is not outstanding, though there are one or two examples of the circular staircase towers popular in Murat, and the church is unremarkable, but as a whole it typifies French village living. Its only claim to fame is the visit made in 1637 by Anne of Austria, wife of Louis XIII, who came to see the miraculous statue of the Virgin then kept in the little Chapel of Notre Dame de Consolation above the village. The statue is now kept in the parish church.

Thiézac is readily accessible by car, but public transport by road or rail is not very conveniently timed for walkers, and the station is more than a kilometre from the village. Nevertheless, it is a good place to stay, since it gives easy access to some of the best walking in the area. In addition, it has now acquired the status of a *village vert*, which means it may be expected to become even more attractive to visitors in the future. The Épicerie also operates a taxi service.

Of the six hotels, L'Elancèze, which is particularly recommended, and Le Casteltinet have two star rating, the Hôtel du Commerce and La Belle Vallée have one star, while Au Combelou and Bellevue are ungraded. Thiézac's key location on an important road means that other accommodation is available locally, a list being available at the Tourist Office in the village. There are well-patronised restaurants at the first two of the hotels named, and a café near the church. In addition, there is a Ferme-Auberge at La Grange Basse, which specialises in regional dishes, though this is in rather a remote situation some five kilometres from Thiézac beyond the village of Salilhes.

The village also boasts its own municipal camp site, set by the river, and there is a *Gîte d'Étape* at nearby Lafont. There are a few small shops, one of which is a Fromagerie, fittingly, as Thiézac was formerly renowned for its cheese. The local speciality was the manufacture of the Auvergne *fromage bleu*, a cheese matured in much the same way as the more famous Roquefort but, unlike the latter, not made exclusively from ewe's milk.

Walk 7   Pas des Rocs

Map:	IGN 1:25000 2435 Ouest, Thiézac et Puy Mary
Time:	2¹/₂ hours walking
Grade:	Easy
Ascent:	300 metres

A steady climb of 300 metres takes you to a high viewpoint, from which there is a long and gentle descent.

The Walk

Start from the church at the west end of Thiézac.

Take the turning which leaves the main street alongside the Hotel du Commerce. It is signposted to the Pas des Rocs and waymarked in yellow. The route follows the upper street of the village, going eastwards, parallel to the main road, for a kilometre to the farm of Laubret. The meadows here, on a south-facing slope, are full of wild flowers, with Ox-eye Daisies, Scabious, Bistort and Cranesbill prominent, but the Carthusian Pink also being found. The small size of the fields makes it imperative that none of the hay crop is wasted, and it is still the normal practice to cut the last swathe up to the hedge or wall by hand, using a scythe. Just after Laubret the track divides, and you follow the hard track on the left as it climbs, with many twists and turns, below an overhanging cliff. Before reaching the topmost crag of the Pas des Rocs, the way cuts through the solid rock, presumably a natural cleft which has been widened to permit the passage of carts, and enters a narrow valley from which there are good views down to the village of Lagoutte and across to the cliff of Casteltinet.

The track soon crosses the stream and climbs the opposite slope to a point under La Bastide where the way divides. Ignore the track ahead to Le Clout in favour of the path that doubles back to the right, rounding a promontory and giving good views of the upper valley of the Cère. Continue climbing past the farm of La Bastide to reach a wider track about half a kilometre further on, where you turn left. This high plateau of La Jarrige is largely used as a cattle pasture, relatively few sheep being kept in this area nowadays. The

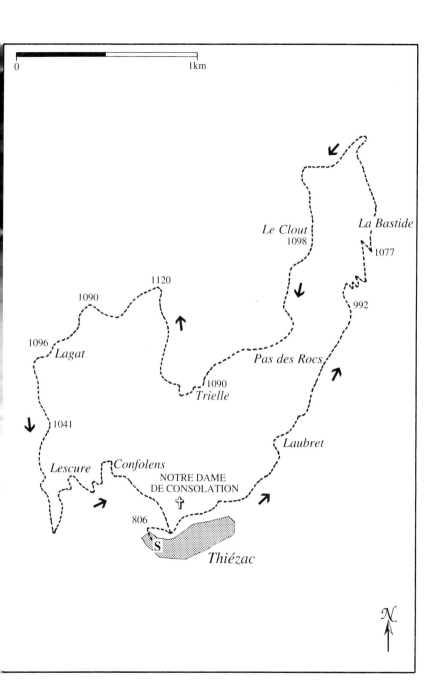

0   1km

La Bastide

Le Clout
1098

1077

1120

1090

992

1096
Lagat

Pas des Rocs

1090
Trielle

1041

Laubret

Lescure   *Confolens*

NOTRE DAME
DE CONSOLATION
✝

806

S

Thiézac

𝒩

predominant breed is the red Salers cow which has a rough, hairy coat. The cows thrive under hard conditions, and much of their early popularity came from their ability to work as draught animals as well as producing a useful milk yield. Pairs of them can still be seen on some of the more remote farms of the Auvergne, hauling a mowing machine by means of a primitive form of head harness. Their fame though, seems to have been spread by the son of a mayor of the town of Salers who, in 1853, promoted an annual show for the breed. You can now enjoy an easy, mostly downhill, walk, with splendid views, as you follow the road round the head of three small valleys, past Le Clout and Trielle, on a surprisingly devious route in the general direction of Thiézac.

At Lagat a *Grande Randonnée* turns off right, but you continue down for another kilometre or so until, at a sign to the hamlet of Lescure, you leave the road by turning back to the left. Just short of the first house of Lescure you double back to the right down a green path beside a hedge. The path looks set to continue straight into Thiézac, but after a little more than 100 metres you must turn left, down a none-too-obvious footpath which crosses the stream below a waterfall and passes a house on the left. From here the general direction is obviously downhill, though it entails first a left turn then two right turns, towards that part of the village east of the parish church. Soon you cross a little village green on the upper street of Thiézac. At the last turning but one, however, it is worth stepping aside for a few minutes to visit the little chapel of Notre Dame de Consolation, shaded by lime trees. It achieved its moment of historical fame in the 17th century, when its statue of the Virgin, now in the church of Thiézac, was visited by Anne of Austria for nine days of prayer, in the hope that its miraculous properties would help produce an heir for her husband, Louis XIII.

Walk 8   L'Elancèze

Map:	IGN 1:25000 2435 Ouest, Thiézac et Puy Mary
Time:	6 hours walking
Grade:	Moderate
Ascent:	770 metres

A long walk, but a very gentle climb, to one of the best viewpoints and most interesting summits in the area.

The Walk

Start from the church at Thiézac.

Leave the main road of the village, near the church, by taking the turning alongside the Hôtel du Commerce, signposted to L'Elancèze. Follow the road eastwards for only 100 metres before turning left, up the hill, at the little village green. At the next junction turn to the left, to the left again at the signpost to Confolens, then to the right. The footpath crosses the stream below the cliff, doubles back, then climbs to join a more major track. Turn right to emerge on a lane south-west of Lescure. Turn left here and climb gently to the road where you turn right. This road is well-graded, and is easily followed for more than a kilometre to reach Lagat. Here you turn left up the *Grande Randonnée*, which is waymarked in red and white and signposted to the Col de Lagat and L'Elancèze. At the col, turn right after crossing the fence by the building, and continue to climb up the stony path which passes to the right of the rocks above.

The character of the landscape now changes, from enclosed fields to open heathland, with bracken, broom, and masses of tall yellow gentians. Soon you see *burons* ahead, but you leave them on your right by following a deeply-worn track to the left, rather overgrown to begin with, but soon becoming a good track. The 'official' route follows the track until it enters the woodland but, in the interests of crossing the wire fence at the most convenient place, leave the track by turning half-right some 200 metres short of the wood, and cut across the heath, with no clear path, to cross the fence at the point where you are politely requested to *fermez le passage S.V.P.* The way ahead is now clear,

51

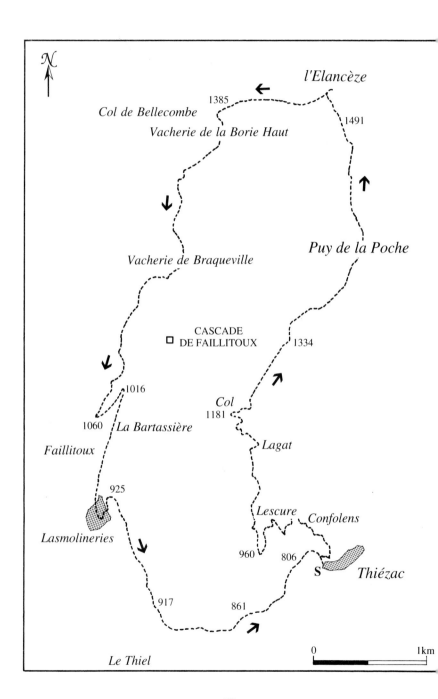

N

l'Elancèze

1385

Col de Bellecombe

1491

Vacherie de la Borie Haut

Vacherie de Braqueville

Puy de la Poche

CASCADE
DE FAILLITOUX

1334

1016

Col
1181

1060   La Bartassière

Faillitoux

Lagat

925

Lescure   Confolens

Lasmolineries

960   806

S   Thiézac

917   861

Le Thiel

0   1km

52

following the path up the slopes of Puy de la Poche, with a fence on the right. The views looking back as you climb are immense, seeming to encompass, on the right day, the whole of south-west France. Soon the path starts to swing left, leaving the fence and heading for the crag south of L'Elancèze, but passing just below it to reach a little pass. Here you start the final climb to the rocky coxcomb which forms the summit. From the top there is a splendid panorama comprising most of the mountains of Cantal, from Puy Mary in the north round to Plomb du Cantal in the east, but dominated by the nearby, and superbly-shaped, peak of Puy Griou.

One of the best parts of the walk is still to come, for the next kilometre of westward-leading ridge is a delight. The route alternates between quite airy rocky sections, with good views of the Jordanne valley below, and small copses of gnarled and twisted beeches. Eventually, it is time to leave the ridge, following the waymarked route (red and white bars) off to the left, on the south side of the ridge, down to the ruined Vacherie de la Borie Haut. A good track starts from here and meanders, first at the woodland edge, then among beech woods, to emerge on the cow pasture of the Vacherie de Braqueville. The deep valley, which has been on your left since the upper *vacherie*, now disappears from view as the track swings westward. A wet section in the woods here is readily avoided by entering the woodland to the left of the track. When the valley reappears it is considerably enhanced by the cliff of Faillitoux. After leaving the woodland you join a road above La Bartassière. Turn left and follow it down. After a hairpin bend you have a choice of two routes. If you take the track which doubles back on the left immediately before La Bartassière you can visit the Cascade de Faillitoux, and continue by a footpath, waymarked in red and white, back to the Col de Lagat to rejoin the outward route. Since this entails a climb of some 170 metres, however, and a subsequent descent, it is not likely to be a universally popular choice. The alternative is to continue down the road to the village of Lasmolineries, following the road round to the left, ignoring a right turn to Le Theil, to cross the bridge. Continue along the road, which descends gently to a fork where the road to Lagat goes left. Go right, turning left along a footpath 200 metres further on, where the road swings right. Follow this path to emerge on the main road just short of the village of Thiézac.

L'Elancèze

Walk 9   Puy Griou

Map:	IGN 1:25000 2435 Est, Murat et Plomb du Cantal
Time:	4$^1/_2$ hours walking
Grade:	Moderate, strenuous on the final scramble
Ascent:	550 metres

Puy Griou, at 1690 metres, is the highest Cantal summit included in this group of walks. It is also steep and rocky on every side, but for this very reason is an exceptionally attractive mountain. It is however possible to by-pass the peak – if the weather should turn bad while on the way, for example.

The Walk

Start from the railway station at Le Lioran, or the car park on the main road 100 metres south-west of the station. Le Lioran is extremely easy to reach by road or rail from Murat, Thiézac, or Vic-sur-Cère, and is a popular centre for walks in summer and ski-ing in winter. Its popularity has rather changed its character, but this cannot detract from the pleasure of climbing Puy Griou, a mountain which, unlike Plomb du Cantal, is difficult to spoil.

To reach the peak, turn left along the main road, past the chapel, and take the right fork. Though now much widened to form the access road to the ski-centres, this was the original high-level pass on the road between Murat and Aurillac. Because it was frequently blocked by snow in winter, it was replaced as early as 1847 by a tunnel, cut entirely by hand and at the expense of many deaths and injuries to the workmen. The railway tunnel, cut ten years later, actually lies below the road tunnel. Some 300 metres from the fork, you arrive at the new ski-village of Font d'Alagnon. Turn right, then fork left after 200 metres to drop down to the Alagnon river.

Just before the bridge, turn right through the car park, an alternative starting point for those arriving by road, and follow the track by the side of the ski-tow, passing just below the new wedge-shaped chalets. Now follow what begins as a broad track through flower-filled meadows, passing close to the bottom of the chair lift on your left. The track continues as a narrower,

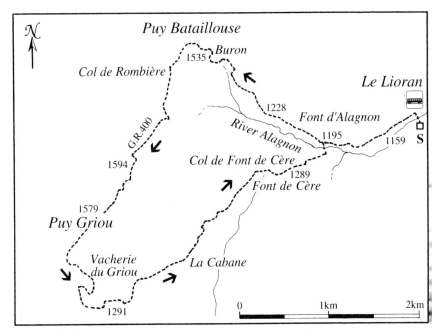

Puy Bataillouse

Col de Rombière

1535 Buron

Le Lioran

1228

Font d'Alagnon

G.R.400

River Alagnon

1195

1159 S

1594

Col de Font de Cère

1289

Font de Cère

1579

Puy Griou

Vacherie du Griou

La Cabane

1291

0   1km   2km

but still clear, path climbing gently along the middle of the valley. When you reach a forestry road turn right for a few metres, then go left up a well-graded track. At the first junction turn left, pass under the barrier, and continue to climb, first through woodland, then across open pasture, until you reach a *buron*, part of which is kept open as a mountain refuge. From the *buron* the path goes to the right of the little rocky knoll above, then turns to climb more directly towards the crest of Puy Bataillouse. On reaching a cross-track, which passes well below the summit, turn left to reach the Col de Rombière, where you pass through a fence by using that extreme rarity in the Auvergne, a swing gate.

Turn left along a clear path which passes west of a small knoll, then go through the fence and walk east of a further summit, before reaching a path junction. Turn right, following the orange waymarks along a narrow path which climbs to the col north-east of Puy Griou. From here there is only 100 metres to climb to the peak, which can be reached either by going straight up the ridge, or by following the path right then turning left up a prominent rocky rib. In either case it is an easy scramble to the surprisingly-extensive summit, with its views across the upper Cère valley to the Plomb du Cantal, and down the precipitous eastern face to the Vacherie du Griou.

To reach the *vacherie*, however, you need to follow the south-west ridge

Puy Griou

down. Alternatively, if you omitted the summit, you can reach the same point by retracing your steps for 100 metres from the col, then continuing by the path which descends round the northern side of Puy Griou. Leave the waymarked path just after entering the woods, turning left at a clearing and following a track just below the top edge of the woodland, which descends gently to the Vacherie du Griou. In either case, having arrived at the hut, you descend slightly to find a track which begins at a gate in the wall to the west. Follow this track as it twists its way down to join a broader, bulldozed track.

Turn left along this track, following it down. Where the track forks, the right-hand branch dipping down to the village of Les Chazes, you continue left at the same level. Go past a barn above La Cabane, and then climb gently on a track parallel to, and just above, the road. This part of the route is delightfully easy and has good views across to Puy du Rocher and Plomb du Cantal. Eventually you reach the Col de Font de Cère, where you take the second turn left after passing the hotel, following white and red waymarks downhill. The road is reached at a hairpin bend: leave it again immediately, continuing to follow the path down. The path takes you down to a road in the valley bottom, where you turn left to arrive back at the bridge over the Alagnon, and rejoin the outward route.

Walk 10   Puy Bataillouse

Map:	IGN 1:25000 2435 Est, Murat et Plomb du Cantal
Time:	5 hours walking
Grade:	Moderate
Ascent:	530 metres

A great ridge walk, with no large changes of level once it is reached. The descent from the final summit is rocky and steep if descended directly, but this short section can be by-passed.

The Walk

Start from the railway station at Le Lioran, or one of the many lay-bys on the main road, all of which are available for car parking.

This walk, like the previous one to Puy Griou, is readily accessible either from east or west. On leaving the station, turn right, down the main road towards Murat. It is only 10 minutes walk, downhill, but it can seem longer if the road is busy. In that case it may be preferable to keep off the road as far as possible by using the lay-bys on the south side. Take the second turning on the left, one kilometre from the station, up a broad track. Follow the track up, with no major turnings to look out for, past a few immensely tall and solitary pines, near to which there is a good view down the Alagnon valley towards Murat.

After $1^1/_2$ kilometres of fairly steady climbing from the road you arrive at a ruined *buron*, its cheese room having a well-insulated barrel-vaulted roof, to keep the cheese cool, while the doorway faces due south to make it hot. It seems illogical, but no doubt it gave the right conditions for ripening the cheeses. At this point the track swings back sharply to the left: follow it past the foot of the high cliff on your right. When a major fork in the track is reached, keep right. The route now climbs a little more steeply, but its line is shaded by beeches and you soon arrive on a beautifully-scented hillside. The gradient is easier now, and there is a splendid view south to the Puy du Rocher.

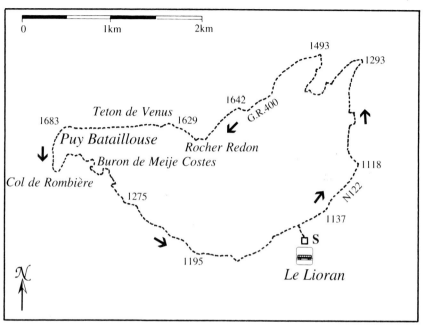

On reaching the rocky spine of the ridge, go left along the skyline to reach a subsidiary summit. Now climb to Rocher Redon, its well-named Eagles Beak crag prominent from here. This is the highest summit of the day, at exactly 1,700 metres, but even here daffodils, Pyrennean Lent Lilies to be precise, bloom in profusion, and the even more showy Yellow Alpine Anemone abounds. The next $2^1/_2$ kilometres of ridge are a delight: the Teton de Venus, followed by a rocky little arête leading to Puy Bataillouse, and a scramble down to the Col de Rombière. The views are among the best in the Auvergne with Puy Mary dominating the view north, Puy Griou that to the west, and the long ridge centred on Plomb du Cantal visible to the south.

The three valleys centred on Puy Bataillouse are as different as could be, the remote and relatively treeless valley of the Santoire to the north contrasting both with the deciduous woods of the Jordanne, to the west, and the largely coniferous woods of the Alagnon, to the south.

The direct descent from Puy Bataillouse to the Col de Rombière is quite exciting, with a rocky scramble on the crest of the ridge. This can, however, be by-passed. On reaching the Col, which is no more than a slight indentation in the skyline, there is a junction of paths. Follow the path to the left until you are right under the summit of Bataillouse, then take the path descending to the right, towards the *buron*.

Puy Mary, Tête de Venus and Puy Bataillouse

Arriving at the Buron de Meije Costes, keep to the right at the front door – the rear of the building is used as a mountain refuge, and is always open – and descend by easy curves into an area of woodland to reach a forestry road. Turn right for a few paces, then left down a narrow path, which keeps below the woods on the hillside to your left, before descending into the middle of the valley and passing near the foot of a chair lift. It now follows more or less the same line, just below the new wedge-shaped chalets, before descending beside a ski tow to reach the bridge over the Alagnon. Turn left to pass through the shopping area of the ski village, and go left again on reaching the road which crosses the pass (the D67). A short descent takes you to the main road (the N122), where a last left turn takes you back to the station.

Saint-Flour

A principal route from Paris to Barcelona, the N9, passes through the low town by the river, so that many visitors are attracted to the ancient and attractive upper town, of some 10,000 inhabitants. There is, consequently, no shortage of accommodation or of places to eat, the principal hotels being L'Europe, Les Voyageurs, Le Nord and Les Roches. The first two have well-recommended restaurants, but the Place d'Armes and the streets leading from it offer a choice of cuisine to suit every pocket. There are three camp sites, the largest of which, the International with 1000 places, lies on the road to Paris and is some distance from the town. Camping des Orgues, a three star site on the outskirts of the upper town, and Camping de l'Ander, a two star site by the river, are much more conveniently placed.

The town takes its name from Florus, a 4th century evangelist who, according to legend, was miraculously enabled to gain access to the formerly impregnable rock. A new town was then sited on the basalt promontory, whose black pillars are best seen from the Avenue des Orgues. The name *orgues* refers to the organ-pipe appearance of the pillars. The best views of the surroundings are, however, to be found at the back of the cathedral, just off the Place d'Armes, where the visitor overlooks precipitous slopes to the north and east, falling away to the River Ander. The cathedral itself is a rather austere, fortress-like church of dark local stone and late-medieval date.

Its main claim to fame is that of being, at 900 meters, the highest cathedral in Europe. The town is much more attractive, with several fine ancient buildings, consistent with its former status as the regional capital of Haute-Auvergne. These include the bishop's palace, which now houses the regional museum, a 15th century governor's house, and a consular house, with a 16th century facade, which houses another museum.

This concern with the past does not mean that the town has no modern role to play, and a certain amount of light industry and new development exists, sensibly located a short distance to the west of the old town, rather than adjoining it. A green belt once separated the two, but this has been eroded to the north of the old town, in the area known as La Fontlong, where new development is taking place. Even so, Saint-Flour remains both an attractive town, and one which is easy to put behind you, with pleasant countryside just a few minutes walk away. The town retains three of its medieval gates and one of them, La Porte des Roches, is used as a way out of the upper town on the first of the walks described here.

Walk 11   St Flour & St Georges

Map:	IGN 1:25000 2535 Est, Saint-Flour
Time:	3 hours walking
Grade:	Easy, but a stiff climb at the end
Ascent:	250 metres

A walk that shows the hilltop site of Saint-Fleurand the neighbouring villages to good advantage.

The Walk

Start from the principal car park of the town, at the western end of the traffic-free area.

From the car park, enter the pedestrian precinct by way of the Rue des Lacs. Any one of several possible side streets will eventually lead you to the cathedral at the east end of the town, the Rue Marchande being perhaps the most direct. The cathedral faces on to a large and attractive square, and at its rear there are good viewpoints looking north and east. From the second of these you descend through the medieval gateway of La Porte des Roches, turning left as soon as possible beyond it down the Chemin des Chevres. There are allegedly 300 steps on the way down to the church of Sainte-Christine, near the old and new bridges across the Ander. From the south end of the new bridge, take the signposted footpath east, crossing a footbridge over a tributary stream and climbing between high hedges with occasional views back to the dramatically-sited upper town. Where the hedged path ends in an open pasture, swing right, following the hedgerow, to join an obvious track up the hill.

On passing beneath the power lines fork right, passing a small quarry on your left, and continue up the hill to join the metalled road near La Chaumette. Go straight ahead rather than turning left, and fork left a little further on, following the road which twists through the hamlet of Bouzengeac. The road soon becomes unfenced and offers good views across this high undulating plateau of woodland, meadow, and rough pasture. Follow the road across the D40, and you will soon be able to turn left into the village of Cousergues. At

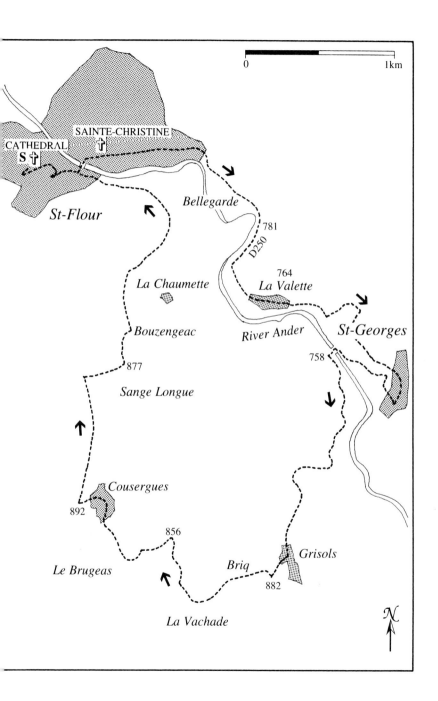

SAINTE-CHRISTINE

CATHEDRAL
S

St-Flour

Bellegarde

781

D250

La Chaumette

764
La Valette

Bouzengeac

River Ander

St-Georges

758

877

Sange Longue

Cousergues

892

856

Briq

Grisols

Le Brugeas

882

La Vachade

N

0   1km

St Georges

the far end is a triangular green, which you pass on your left. Now turn right along the D40. Cousergues appears to be the principal village of this large, breezy, plateau, which you cross by following the D40 for about $1\frac{1}{2}$ kilometres before turning left across the green marking the centre of the dispersed hamlet of Grisols: take the middle road of three left turns in quick succession. Turn left again at the end of the green, following the road northwards. Here you may notice the more Mediterranean character of the houses, which results from their use of red clay tiles rather than the grey slates of Cantal.

From Grisols, the road descends in wide, sweeping bends to the river, giving views of the Ander valley, the twin villages of St Michel and St Georges on their respective hilltops, and the Margeride uplands in the far distance. Cross the bridge over the river, and the road beyond (the D250), taking, instead, the uphill road to St Georges, where refreshments are available at the Auberge du Chevalier St George. Turn sharp left here, and when you reach the wooden Crucifix at the end of the village fork left along the waymarked GR footpath (red and white bars). The path passes through fields, with views down to the valley, then goes along the woodland edge, before joining a farm track which becomes a metalled road leading to La Valette. Here you join the D250, and follow it, right, along the riverside, to join the main road back to the river bridge and the climb to the upper town.

Walk 12   Andelat

Map:	IGN 1:25000 2535 Est, Saint-Flour
Time:	3 hours walking
Grade:	Easy
Ascent:	100 metres

A walk from Saint-Flour, featuring the gently-rolling countryside of the upper Ander alley.

The Walk

Start from the Georges Pompidou monument at the northern end of Saint-Flour's principal car park.

From the monument, turn west for a few paces then take the lower of the two roads which leave the town side by side. This is known as the Rue Blaise Pascal, and you follow it steeply down past the college. Go straight across at the crossroads, staying with the same road, which has now turned east towards the river. About 200 metres beyond the crossroads turn left. This area is under development, and landmarks are in the process of changing, but in 1990 the turning you take was a newly-cut road with a large signboard at the top announcing building plots for sale. In any event, the turning is at the top of a steep-sided and very rural little valley, which hopefully will survive the present expansion. Follow the new road down for 100 metres or so, then turn off right, just before the first of the new houses, down an old hedged green track, which passes below them.

The track takes you to a road opposite a house: turn right and, after 200 metres, fork left down a lane leading, in half a kilometre, to a railway crossing with an automatic barrier. Continue down the lane beyond, going parallel to the river, which is crossed by means of the wooden bridge at Massales mill, a very quiet and rural spot, in spite of it being such a short distance from all the bustle of Saint-Flour. Turn left behind the house and follow a hedged track near the river to Roueyre. Note that the name has inexplicably been omitted from the IGN 1:25000 map, through it is present on their smaller scale maps.

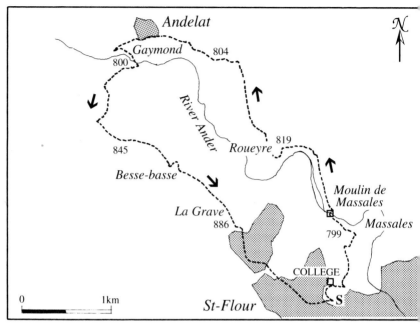

You emerge on a loose gravelled track and follow it left for 200 metres before crossing the main road (the D679). After a few paces, turn right along a second, parallel, road and climb the hill for about 300 metres, passing two turnings to the left. Just past a house, the road divides: take the left turn, still climbing up the hill. From the brow you get a good view forward to the distant mountains of Cantal. Ignoring a sandy track going off to the left, keep going along a pleasant roughly-surfaced route that heads north. Teasels grow alongside the way and it climbs gently to a hilltop, with a view back to Saint-Flour as well as forward to the church of Andelat.

A left turn soon afterwards takes you down and across a stream. Beyond, the way climbs again to arrive on a metalled road just below the massive churchyard wall of Andelat. Here go straight ahead, down the road, though the church itself is well worth seeing if you first make the short detour to the right. Returning to the junction, follow the road as it drops fairly steeply down to the valley. There, turn left along the main road for a short distance in order to cross the River Ander again.

Take the road on the right immediately after the bridge, and follow it for 400 metres before turning left up a track which crosses the railway line at another automatic barrier. Turn right directly afterwards to reach a junction after about 150 metres. Turn left on a stony track that swings left after a short

Andelat church

distance, becoming a narrow path between wire fences heading east across a low ridge. Having crossed the ridge, the hedges resume during the short descent to a farm track.

Turn left and follow the track down to the old farm of Besse-Basse, turning right in front of the house. Keep straight ahead when the access track to the farm doubles back to the left, the way forward being a loose, sandy track leading over the ridge ahead and giving good views back long the Ander valley. After passing a barn on the left at La Grave, and a timber yard on the right, you will arrive at a crossroads. Go straight across into a new road, the Rue Fernand Vert. At the end, turn left and go along the Avenue de Besserette, past the Fire Station and the Gendarmerie, to arrive back at the Pompidou monument.

La Bourboule

Although La Bourboule has been chosen as the centre for the following walks, they could be done just as well from Le Mont-Dore. The two towns, only 6 kilometres apart, have a great deal in common, both being set in the narrow valley of the upper Dordogne. They are also very conveniently linked, both by road and by rail, with frequent trains to the terminus at Le Mont-Dore. Though both are spa towns of rather similar character, they specialise in different medical conditions. La Bourboule has acquired a reputation for treating allergies, while Le Mont-Dore deals mainly with respiratory problems. These differences are matters of treatment rather than being in the nature of the spa waters.

It appears that the hot springs of this region were known and patronised over 2,000 years ago, for long before the Romans arrived local Gaulish tribes were bathing here, to judge by the remains of baths found by excavation at Le Mont-Dore in 1818. The Romans are thought to have had a much larger building complex than that of the present spa, but the tradition of bathing seems to have fallen into disuse around the 7th century AD, and was not revived for nearly a thousand years. In the 16th century, when spas throughout Europe became popular again, Vichy was predominant in France, although it is likely that the springs of the upper Dordogne gained at least a local reputation. Certainly by the 19th century they were well patronised. In recent years the number of visitors arriving for winter sports has greatly exceeded the number seeking thermal treatment.

Le Mont-Dore, being 200 metres higher than La Bourboule, has a slight advantage for winter sports enthusiasts in terms of snowfall, and a considerable advantage in having a funicular to the summit of Puy de Sancy, the highest point in central France. This operates in summer too, ensuring that the peak is rarely free of visitors, and even helping, perhaps, to limit the number of people to be found on other summits in the area.

In terms of the accommodation offered by the two places, both the number and the standard of hotels and restaurants is comparable. At La Bourboule the hotels du Louvre and du Parc are the two largest, and each has a two star rating. Les Isles Brittaniques has three stars and, in addition, there are several one star hotels, together with pensions and apartments. If you prefer to stay outside the town itself, there are many small hotels and pensions in nearby villages. The town is very well provided with camp sites, no less than seven being available, ranging from the three star Les Clarines to the *Aire Naturelle*, or unsophisticated, facilities of Les Pradelloux.

Walk 13   Roche de Vendeix

Map:	IGN 1:25000 2432 Est, La Bourboule et Mont-Dore
Time:	3 hours walking
Grade:	Easy
Ascent:	320 metres

An easy introductory walk from this centre, to the legendary stronghold of a local brigand.

The Walk

Start from the centre of La Bourboule.

Leave the town by following the minor road that heads east along the north bank of the river. After $1^1/_2$ kilometres the road makes a small detour round the back of a farm equipment suppliers, before emerging on to the main road (the D130) opposite a track signposted to Les Cascades. Cross the road and follow this hazel-hedged track as it becomes a deep hollow way climbing through woodland. Ignore a green path going off to the left, opposite a turning to the rather insignificant lower falls, and continue to a fork, where you bear right. The track now becomes a shelf, set high above the valley on the right, and reaches the chalet that provides access, for a small charge, to the upper falls, or Cascade du Plat a Barbe. From the chalet take the long-distance footpath waymarked in red and white, which is signposted to Le Mont-Dore and the mountains beyond.

The track soon turns downhill and crosses the stream at a pole bridge. Here you change direction, climbing to the south-west on a clearly-waymarked path among tall pines, usually to the accompaniment of bird song. The track soon levels out and reaches Le Gibeaudet. Turn left at the first house, going up a steep, narrow, path signposted to the Puy de Sancy. With an easier objective in mind, you follow the path, which emerges on a track taking you straight ahead. The way is now shaded by beeches and gives fine views south-west towards the crag of Le Capucin, above Le Mont-Dore, and the high green ridge of Puy de l'Angle. On arriving at the open common of Chamablanc,

69

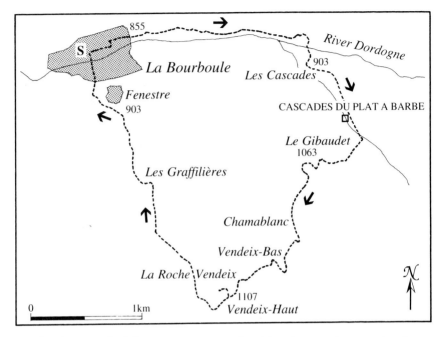

take the second of the two turnings on the right, the one signposted to La
Roche Vendeix. The heath here is bright with yellow broom and giant yellow
gentians, the latter a locally-prolific plant whose roots are distilled to produce
an alcohol used either as an aperitif or to flavour Schnaps.

Follow the track down to the hamlet of Vendeix-Bas. Turn left, heading
directly for La Roche ahead. A cottage on the left has the steeply-pitched roof
and fish-scale slates which are characteristic of the area, though the thin
slates used here seem to be a relatively modern substitute for the traditional,
and much thicker, split stones known as *lauzes*. When the lane turns left, go
straight ahead, descending to cross a road, then the stream at a footbridge.
Climb up a shady lane beyond to reach the hamlet of Vendeix-Haut, turning
right immediately before the first house along a signposted path to the rocky
summit, with its 'organ-pipes' of columnar basalt. Though ringed by higher
hills, the outcrop of La Roche still manages to dominate its immediate
surroundings like a medieval castle. It may well be that it was once fortified,
as there are building foundations on the north side of the rock, and it has the
reputation of having once been the stronghold of a notorious local brigand,
Aimerigot Marcheix. It would have been easy to defend, but is not a good
viewpoint because of the surrounding hills. An exception is the view north,
where La Bourboule appears to be only a stone's throw away.

Roche de Vendeix

Return to Vendeix-Haut along the same path, turning right through the hamlet then keeping straight ahead down the footpath signposted to La Bourboule. This soon becomes a track beside a stream, then a metalled road: continue to follow it, ignoring two turnings off to the right, to the hamlet of Les Graffilières. Just before the first building, turn left down a green track, then go right at the foot of the slope, along a track which becomes a road. Follow the road to its junction with the D88 at the village of Fenestre. Turn left along the D88 and in a few minutes you will find yourself back in La Bourboule.

Walk 14   Col de Guery

Map:	IGN 1:25000 2432 Est, La Bourboule et Mont-Dore
Time:	6 hours walking
Grade:	Moderate
Ascent:	660 metres

A moderate climb to the viewpoint of Puy Gros, then easy walking to Lac de Guery and the spectacular view from Col de Guery. The return route passes the base of La Banne d'Ordanche, whose summit can be reached by a short climb.

The Walk

Start from the roadside parking area for Les Cascades, by the D130, 1$^1/_2$ kilometres west of La Bourboule.

Cross the road and the bridge over the river, skirt the rear of the industrial building on your left, and turn right up a lane which crosses the railway and a new road. The lane climbs to the hamlet of Les Planches. Go straight ahead here, across the D996, but after 50 metres turn right up an old track, through shady beech woods, which leads into flower-filled meadows. Now turn left along a lane to Lusclade. Go through the hamlet and continue eastwards, ignoring a track on the right heading towards Le Mont-Dore in favour of the left branch, which climbs to enter a beech wood on the flanks of Puy Gros.

Though the climb is steep, the woodland provides welcome shade, and when you emerge from the trees the gradient eases, the track doubling back to the right between broken stone walls. Just before a wire fence is reached, turn right, through the wall, at a waymark, passing a ruined *buron*. Now climb gently to the pass between Puy Gros and Le Tenon. Turn right here and follow an easy path along the ridge, with views back to the dramatic cliff of La Banne d'Ordanche, to the summit of Puy Gros.

Despite its appearance from below, the mountain behind the escarpment

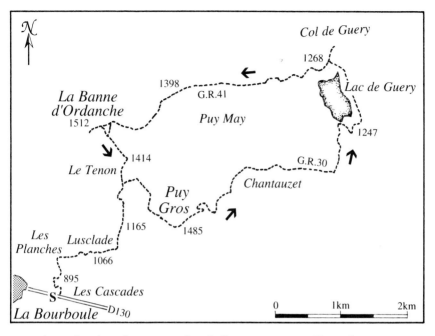

is almost level, and is carpeted with flowers in spring. From the summit,
follow the path which heads north-east, following the red and white
waymarks and ignoring the path descending southwards to Le Mont-Dore.
The way heads for a barn and a ruined house standing in a cow-pasture, but
just short of a fence you turn sharply left, following the fence to the point
where three fences intersect. Cross the fence coming in from the left, and
follow a path that sweeps in a clockwise direction around Puy de Chantauzet.
Cross a broken fence, then a complete one, at another point where three
fences meet. Cross the low rocky ridge ahead and continue with a wire fence
on your right, passing a conifer plantation, to reach a cross track coming from
a barn on your right. Turn left along this into a wood. Follow the forest track
to the Lac de Guery, one of the two sources of the River Dordogne, where you
turn right to reach a road, the D983.

There is, unfortunately, no alternative to following the D983, which can
be quite a busy road, to reach the Col de Guery. So go left, passing a café and
a stall selling rocks and fossils by way of compensation. At the Col, there is
a car park with a splendid view of the valley towards Rochefort Montagne,
seen between the twin crags of Roche Tuilière and Roche Sanadoire, the
latter the site of a fortress until the 15th century.

Leaving the Col, take the track heading south-west, passing a map showing

Roche Sanadoire

cross-country ski-ing trails in the area ahead. The roughly-surfaced road leads to a deserted farm, after which the route continues in the same direction on a green lane between wire fences, heading for the impressive peak of La Banne.

At the pass near the foot of the peak, go through the wicket gate on the left, then make a choice. You can either climb the crag and return or, alternatively, turn left downhill immediately. In the latter case, you follow the fence to the corner, then turn left along the clear track from La Banne which will lead you to the green ridge of Le Tenon. Turn right here, and follow the crest of the ridge to a small outcrop of rocks. There the path turns left and descends to the *buron* noted on the outward journey. Just before reaching it, cross a broad track heading west before rejoining the outward route which you follow down through the woods to Lusclade, Les Planches, and the starting point on D130.

Walk 15   Puy de l'Angle

Map:	IGN 1:25000 2432 Est, La Bourboule et Mont-Dore
Time:	6 hours walking
Grade:	Moderate, with two steep climbs
Ascent:	750 metres

A long and scenic walk, the Puy de l'Angle at 1738 metres being merely the highest of several summits. However, the walk as a whole traverses fine country and includes two impressive waterfalls.

The Walk

Start from the railway station at Le Mont-Dore, conveniently reached by frequent trains from La Bourboule, or the adjacent car parking area.

Leaving the station by way of the Avenue Guyot Desaigne, turn right at the top, along the Avenue des Belges. Follow this as far as the Thermal Baths, turning left up the street immediately beyond. After 100 metres, just past the Hotel Europe, turn left again up a flight of steps. The path now climbs through woodland to arrive at a level footpath known as the Chemin de Melchi-Rose, which you follow, to the right, to reach the D36. Cross the road here and follow the path to the left, signposted to La Grande Cascade, that goes just above the road. The route twists and turns upwards, first through beech woods then through pines, with frequent gaps permitting views towards Puy de Sancy, on its way to the great overhanging cliff over which the waterfall plunges.

Cross the footbridge at its foot and continue upwards to gain good views of the top of the fall. On arriving at the plateau do not cross the stream again: instead turn right, crossing open heathland with scattered rowans and springtime cuckoos, before turning left across the head of the stream to reach the road near the Col de la Croix St Robert. Cross the road at the sheepfold and head due north for the little pass between Puy de Mareilh and Puy de l'Angle. There turn right to climb to the latter summit. This steep climb

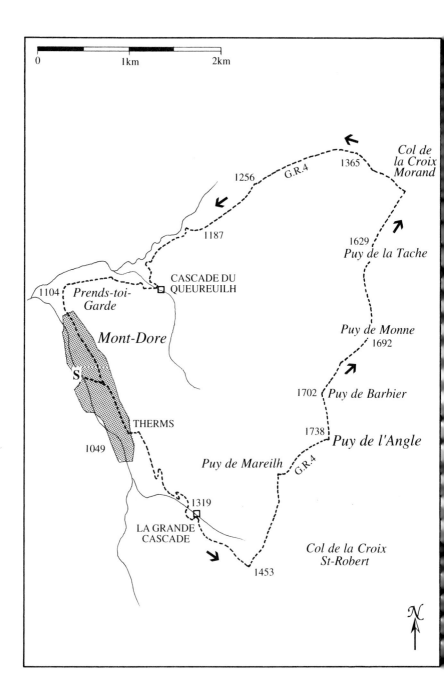

0   1km   2km

1256   G.R.4   1365   Col de
                          la Croix
                          Morand

1187   1629
                          Puy de la Tache

1104   Prends-toi-   CASCADE DU
        Garde   QUEUREUILH

Mont-Dore

                          Puy de Monne
                          1692

S   1702 Puy de Barbier

THERMS   1738
                          Puy de l'Angle
1049   Puy de Mareilh   G.R.4

1319

LA GRANDE
CASCADE   Col de la Croix
                          St-Robert
        1453

N

affords ample opportunities to turn and admire the views back to the slightly higher, and much more popular, summits centred on Puy de Sancy. After arriving at the top, which you are likely to have to yourself, turn left and descend gently to Puy de Barbier before continuing to the Puy de Monne.

This mountain, an almost perfect cone seen end-on, proves to have a rocky little ridge which the path traverses. The views are superb in every direction, that to the east being down towards Lac Chambon. The ridge continues north over an un-named summit to Puy de la Tache, with an abundance of wild flowers throughout, including alpine daffodils in early summer. After three splendid kilometres it is then necessary to descend alongside the derelict ski-tow to reach the road at the Col de la Croix Morand. Turn left here for 300 metres, leaving the road by a path to the right just before a track turns off right, so as to cross the track and pass through the fence at a signpost to Le Mont-Dore. The path is clear as it crosses a cow pasture, then traverses a heathy area with occasional boggy patches, home to a wide variety of wild flowers including orchids. The newly-planted conifers to either side of the path may, unfortunately, be about to change the ecology of this delightful area.

The grassed but obvious track which continues the line of the path hereabouts appears to be a former highway to the col, though you soon reach a farm road and turn left along it, going through woodland to reach the main road (the D983). Go straight across, following the path into mixed woodland where it again becomes clear that this was the old highway. After emerging from the woodland, the way turns sharply left at a point which is clearly waymarked. It then turns right to follow the course of the nearby stream westwards. On arriving at a road-end, with a small car park for visitors to the waterfalls, turn left along a waymarked track and go over a bridge to the Cascade du Queureuilh. Though not as impressive as La Grande Cascade, this fall does have the advantage of being lit by the afternoon sun. Turn left on leaving the fall and, on emerging into a lane, turn right. Keep straight ahead at the next junction. The road now takes you directly to the oddly-named hamlet of Prends-toi-Garde, where you continue towards Le Mont-Dore. By taking the left fork, then going straight ahead on reaching the main road, you will arrive just above the station at the top of the Avenue Guyot Desaigne, where the walk began.

La Grande Cascade

Walk 16   Le Capucin and the Montagne de Bozat

Map:	IGN 1:25000 2432 Est, La Bourboule et Mont-Dore
Time:	5 hours walking
Grade:	Moderate
Ascent:	550 metres

A steep climb at the beginning of this route is followed by a long, easy, walk. Some of the climb can be avoided by taking the funicular if it is working. Two alternatives are given, returning either to Le Mont-Dore or to La Bourboule. A fine variant to the route is to catch a train to Mont-Dore and to walk back to La Bourboule.

The Walk

Start from the Tourist Information Office in Le Mont-Dore. To reach it from the station, turn right outside, then take the first left, going along the Boulevard Mirabeau. Turn right at the fork, along the Avenue Jules Ferry, and you will find the office on your left at the top, just after the crossroads.

Emerging from the Tourist Office, pass through the gardens ahead and cross the road. Turn right along a metalled footpath which passes in front of the Hôtel des Sapins, but is at present un-signposted. The path climbs quite steeply at first, but the gradient then eases and you arrive at a broad terrace known as the Chemin des Artistes, high above the town. Turn right along it for a few paces, then go left up the path signposted as the Chemin des Milles Gouttes. This broad track winds rather more than the previous one, to ease the gradient, and takes you to the top station of the funicular. Here, as you might expect, you ignore the level tracks to left and right, and continue forward up a rocky track which quickly takes you to the Salon du Capucin, where refreshments are available.

Turn left on joining a metalled road here and follow it as it heads south and climbs steadily to a clearing with a superb view of the rocky nose of Le Capucin. Soon the road doubles back to the left to reach a buron, then continues as a grassy track. Follow this as far as a rocky knoll on the ridge

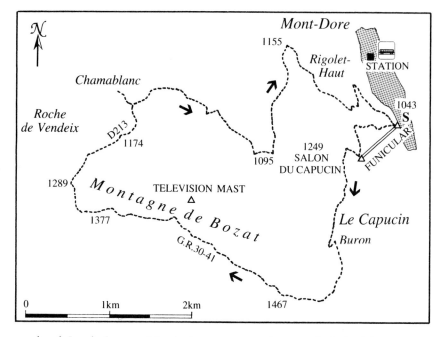

ahead. Just before reaching it there are views down to the left of the upper reaches of the Dordogne, which rises below Puy de Sancy. The track swings to the right to pass round the base of the knoll and reaches a plateau with extensive views to the east. Those to the west are, however, cut off by a rocky ridge in the near distance, the Montagne de Bozat, your next destination.

To reach it, leave the main track to Puy de Sancy by turning right near a small reservoir on top of the knoll and follow the red and white waymarks westward. You can now enjoy more than 3 kilometres of ridge-top walking at a height of between 1,400 and 1,500 metres with fine views back to the serrated skyline adjoining Puy de Sancy, and immeasurably distant views forward into Limousin. The whole of this Montagne de Bozat is bright with daffodils and the white form of the Alpine Anemone in May, and although the path is not particularly well-trodden, the direction is clear and there are good waymarks: go past the television mast, away to your right, and through a fence, before making an abrupt left turn down into a cow pasture with a buron. Soon you join the track which serves the buron, and the way is now broad and clear, leading through a new conifer plantation to reach an old wood which has been felled and apparently left to regenerate naturally.

From here there is a fine view down to La Bourboule and you can, if you wish, descend to it from here. But whether La Bourboule or Mont-Dore is

Le Capucin

A distant view of Le Capucin

your destination you need to follow the track a little further, descending quite steeply through mature woodland now, and going straight ahead at a junction of tracks. Very soon afterwards you will find yourself within a few yards of a road (the D213) and it is best to turn right along it, since the forest track which should turn right here is blocked further on by fallen trees and is evidently little used. After rather less than a kilometre of road you arrive at a junction. Turn left for 200 metres to reach Chamablanc, if you are bound for La Bourboule, turning left again there and following the route described in Walk 11 towards La Roche Vendeix.

For Le Mont-Dore, on the other hand, you follow the road forward from the junction, losing 70 metres of height on the descent to the bridge, but regaining most of it on the subsequent ascent. As some compensation, however, there is a fine view back to the Montagne de Bozat. At the next road junction, on the crest of the ridge, turn right, and on reaching the hamlet of Rigolet-Haut take the second turning on the left, above the houses. After 200 metres turn left again, along the *Ancien Chemin de la Tour*, a delightful and shady path through mature woodland. Take the second turning to the left and quickly descend to a broad track, the Chemin des Artistes once again. Turn left and descend to the road. Now turn right to quickly arrive back at the Tourist Information Office in Mont-Dore.

Saint-Nectaire

Saint-Nectaire is situated about 40 kilometres south of Clermont-Ferrand, to which it is linked by coach services. The village has twin claims to fame. It has a quite outstanding Romanesque church, but is perhaps better known as the home of a distinctive cheese, whose manufacture is said to date back to the third century AD. Oddly enough, the cheese is no longer made on any scale in the immediate vicinity, though its method of manufacture is still displayed.

Saint-Nectaire really consists of two quite separate places; le Haut, and le Bas, the former a compact village sited on and around Mont Cornadore, the latter a long straggling place in the valley bottom.

Le Haut has capitalized on its outstanding hilltop situation, crowned by its superb church, which attracts a constant stream of visitors. As a result it is well supplied with restaurants, and even a few hotels of moderate size, such as the Belle-vue and the Bel-air, both one-star, and the Marinette, which is ungraded. The thermal springs of Le Bas claim Roman origins, but its fame as a spa was acquired much later. Though it still has both hotels and baths, like la Bourboule and Le Mont-Dore, it has had to diversify in order to survive. The hotels are larger than those at le Haut: l'Hermitage, le Savoy, and de la Paix are all two-star, while the smaller de Lyon has one star. All the hotels named (except le Savoy) have restaurants, but only the Hôtel de Lyon, the Marinette, and the Hôtel de la Cascade further down the valley, at Saillant, are open all the year. There is a wide range of other accommodation, including four camp sites (one of them at Saillant). The municipal camp site does not open until June.

Nectaire, the Saint for whom the village is named, was an early Christian, whose life and miracles are featured on the capitals of the columns in the church., but whose association with the district is unclear. Certainly he was several thousand years too late to have been responsible for the first foundation of settlement here, for the region abounds in prehistoric remains in the form of standing stones and megalithic tombs. One of the best of these monuments is very close to the village, and is visited on the first walk from this centre.

Walk 17   Megaliths near Saint-Nectaire

Map:	IGN 1:25000 2532 Ouest, Aydat & Saint-Nectaire
Time:	4 hours walking
Grade:	Easy
Ascent:	250 metres

An easy walk to a prominent viewpoint, with opportunities to look at a number of the local prehistoric sites.

The Walk

Start from the lower village of Saint-Nectaire, where the few shops and most of the hotels are sited.

Take the lane heading north-west, signposted to Sapchat and follow it up the hill for a few hundred metres to reach a not very obvious turning to the right. Take this track which descends to pass in front of the former casino, then crosses the main road by way of a small bridge. Turn right beyond the bridge, going up steps and following a winding path to reach a megalithic grave, a dolmen, still impressive in spite of its urban trappings and, mercifully, free from graffiti. This is the best preserved of the local prehistoric monuments and has, perhaps, been reconstructed. On leaving it, continue up the hill to a small viewing tower and turn left along the road above the tennis courts, heading north towards Saint-Nectaire le Haut.

From the road, you soon get a glimpse of the Sancy Massif between the nearer hills, and as you approach the village there is a superb view of the 12th century parish church of Saint-Nectaire, set on its hilltop and flanked by the village houses. Follow the road to the top of the village street and turn right at the footpath sign to Puy de Mazeyres. Turn right again after a few paces (just before emerging on to the D150 road) and follow a broad track which twists its way gently up the hill. Ignore all three turnings to the left and continue to join the road at the top of the hill. Leave it immediately, however, by turning right along another broad track heading towards the TV masts on Puy de Mazeyres.

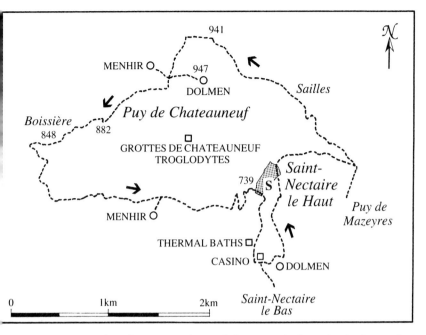

When the track ends continue forward along a path through a little wood to emerge on to a road. Go straight across and take a narrow path that climbs to the orientation table on the summit. The view is splendid, both to the west and the south, but is irretrievably spoiled by the proximity of the masts and the hideous fencing surrounding them. If you are lucky, a buzzard soaring overhead may take your mind off it. Now retrace your steps back across the access road serving the masts, and on to the D150, turning left along it for 600 metres before taking the turning on the right signposted to Les Arnats. On reaching the hamlet of Sailles, turn right, up a metalled road between buildings which soon becomes a track. Ignore turns to left and right until, just after the last buildings, you come to a fork. Turn left, and take the track, which offers excellent views, to rejoin the road you left at Sailles by a disused sandstone quarry.

Now turn right and follow the road as it climbs up the side of a deep valley above Saint-Nectaire. Turn left at the crossroads, and follow D640 for 300 metres before making a left turn along a track signposted to Menhir de Freydefont. Soon you reach the plateau edge: turn right along a track signposted to the Menhir. It is not particularly interesting, however, and you may prefer to turn left, rather than right, to follow a well-worn path eastwards along the crest of the ridge to reach an un-signposted, but rather more

85

The dolmen of Saint-Nectaire

impressive, dolmen. It seems to be of poorer construction than the one at Saint-Nectaire, or perhaps its capstone has slipped. In any event the whole thing is difficult to see among the trees, and fails to make the same impact even if its size is impressive. It certainly makes you wonder who was buried on this exposed ridge, and if the ridge had been cleared of trees, to make the dolmen more visible at that time.

Whether the Menhir or the dolmen has attracted you, you will need to return to the main track, reaching it at the point where it leaves the plateau and starts to descend. As you follow it down, keep to the right when it sweeps to the right, rather than following the branch going to the Chateauneuf caves. The whole hillside here is a patchwork of tiny terraced fields, some in use, some overgrown, but all indicating ancient cultivation. After a kilometre or so you take the left turn when the track forks, and walk with a massively-reinforced lynchet bank on your right to emerge on to the D145. Turn left and follow it for 600 metres to its junction with the main road. Turn right for 150 metres then turn left along a broad track which climbs into mixed woodland. Here there are obviously rich pickings for birds of prey, to judge by the kites and buzzards competing for air space overhead.

The track bends left and continues due east over level ground. About one kilometre after leaving the road, keep left at a fork in the track. After a further

The view from the Puy de Mazeyres

half kilometre you join a track coming in from the right at a clump of pine trees next to a clearing. Here you can, if you wish, make a short detour of 100 metres to the right to reach a prominent standing stone set on a ridge. Retrace your steps to the clump of pines and go forward along what is now a very clear track eastwards. This descends by a twisting route to reach a road and the first houses of Saint-Nectaire. It ought to be possible, by turning right here for one kilometre, to join the D150 and follow it down to the lower village, but there may be a problem with crossing the stream. A better solution is to follow the road to the left, going down to the main road and then turning right along it at least as far as the new thermal baths. Now by turning right across the car park and behind the baths you will find a new footbridge which will take you on to the road to Sapchat (the D150) just above the Casino. From here, retrace your steps to Le Bas.

Walk 18   Château de Murol

Map:	IGN 1:25000 2532 Ouest, Aydat & Saint-Nectaire
Time:	5 hours walking
Grade:	Moderate
Ascent:	320 metres

A long walk, but a straightforward one, with an opportunity to visit the major château of the locality.

The Walk

Start from the lower car park for Saint-Nectaire, at the cross roads on the D996, immediately below the church. If you have not previously visited the church, it is only a few minutes walk up the steps which start at the southern end of the car park. Please note that outside the main holiday times the church is only open to visitors in the afternoons.

Cross the main road and the bridge, taking the minor road which climbs steeply westward. At the top of the hill, opposite the first house, turn right up a track, then go right again after about 100 metres. This track, marked Chemin d'Enchaumie and Croix St Roch, twists and turns, giving good views back to the church, before crossing a plateau and entering a wood. After the first clearing, you reach a fork by a clump of pine trees. They way lies to the right, but a short detour to the left takes you to the crest of a ridge by a prominent standing stone.

The right turn at the fork takes you on to a level track through mixed woodland. Soon you catch your first glimpse of the Château of Murol, just before the track swings right and descends to the main road (D996). Turn left here for 100 metres and, at the top of the hill, turn right, following a track through hay meadows with fine theatrical views of the château and a backdrop of mountains. This section of the walk is part of a long distance footpath, and is marked with the familiar red and white waymarks as it climbs over a shoulder of the prominent hill on the right. The view now becomes truly expansive, for in addition to the château you can see wooded hills

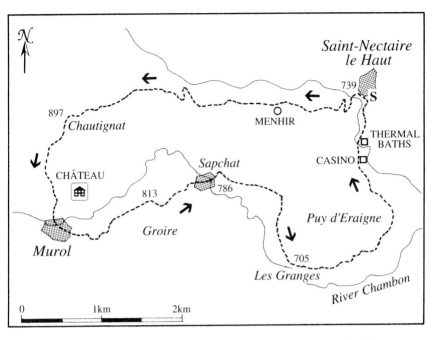

rolling away to the east, and the serrated ridge of the Sancy massif to the west.

On reaching the village of Chautignat, take the first road on the left, and at the bottom of the village keep to the left along a track in the general direction of the château, whose dramatic west face is now well displayed. When you reach a road, keep straight ahead, with the car park on your left. At the top of the hill is the entrance to the château, which is open every day during the summer months and is well worth a visit. Continue down the road towards the village, keeping straight ahead down a minor road at the first bend; and descending to reach the river near a bridge. Cross the river here and take the second turn on the left. At the road junction at the top of the hill go straight on, along the Rue de Groire, following the road for 250 metres before turning left along a broad track.

After 100 metres go straight ahead at a junction of tracks, taking a newly bulldozed route and emerging shortly on to an even more newly-created track that is not shown on IGN maps and which seems to serve the quarries of red volcanic ash on the hill. Turn right along the new track, and immediately after passing the quarries, on your right, go straight across at a junction of four tracks. The way now skirts the base of the hill on the right and emerges on to a road (the D146) north-east of Groire. Turn left, and at the next road junction go left again, to pass through the village of Sapchat. After leaving

Saint-Nectaire

the village you cross two bridges in quick succession. After the second, turn right immediately along a broad track which leaves the river and climbs to a sandy ridge.

A little way along the ridge the track forks: follow yellow waymarkers along the right-hand branch towards Les Granges. This steep, stony track descends past a well-preserved wayside Cross on a rocky promontory. Further on, at the Crucifix in the hamlet of Les Granges, turn left, and when the lane finishes, go forward on a gently-climbing track, still following yellow waymarkers. Soon the track traverses a thinly-wooded plateau, with views down the steep slope of the valley of the Chambon, backwards to the Roche Romaine, the destination for Walk 19, and forwards to Saillant.

Ignoring a track going off to the left, you begin to descend. Fork right on the way down, making another right turn very soon after. This is a slightly confusing area because of recent forestry work, but if you continue in the same direction, and follow the yellow waymarkers, you will arrive at the D150 just above the Casino of lower Saint-Nectaire. To return to the starting point go straight across the D150 and down a track leading to a new footbridge. After crossing the stream, continue behind the thermal baths to reach the baths' car park. Now turn left along the main road back to the crossroads.

Walk 19   La Roche Romaine

Map:	IGN 1:25000 2532 Ouest, Aydat & Saint-Nectaire
Time:	2¹/₂ hours walking
Grade:	Easy
Ascent:	125 metres

A gentle walk in the vicinity of Murol, a small place, overhung by its ancient château, whose origins date back to the 6th century. Like Murat, Murol is said to owe its former importance to its site – in this case at a river crossing where east-west and north-south routes met.

The Walk

Start from the old bridge in the centre of Murol, some five kilometres west of Saint-Nectaire. There is limited car parking near the bridge, but much more space near the Tourist Office, on the southern by-pass.

Head south from the bridge and take the second turning on the left, going up the hill to the road junction at the top. Go straight ahead along the Rue de Groire, follow it for about one kilometre before taking a right fork just past the Hôtel des Dômes. Walk into the old hamlet of Groire and turn right over the stream along the track signposted to Roche de Romaine. After a few twists and turns this track becomes a broad way through woodland, heading south-east along the flank of the Puy de Besolles. There is a rocky section, where fallen boulders litter the route, beyond which the way becomes a narrow, walled, path, then an unfenced path through more woodland, before becoming a clear track again shortly before reaching the Roche Romaine.

It is as well to be aware of the possible confusion arising from the use of the same word, *Roman*, to denote quite different things in French and English. In French, *Roman* refers not to antiquities of the Roman period but, when used as a proper noun, to a particular medieval style based on Roman principles, and characterised, in architecture, by the use of the round arch. It signifies what, in English, is called the Romanesque style, though more often it is called Norman. The French word *Romain*, on the other hand, has

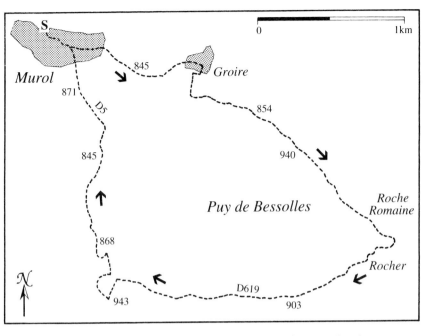

exactly the same meaning as the English 'Roman', and it is used in that sense here, though exactly how this evidently-natural outcrop of rock comes to have any connection with Rome is not clear.

It is nevertheless an interesting feature, and a fine viewpoint. There is also a well-preserved wayside Cross about 100 metres away on the crest of the same ridge. Follow the track forward as it swings to the right into the hamlet of Rocher, turning left at the water troughs. Almost immediately turn right, and keep right at the fork by the last houses. The road follows a terrace and leads to the D619. Turn right and enjoy a fine vista towards Les Monts-Dore. The hillside to your right is a mass of tiny cultivation terraces, all long-since disused and totally overgrown. At the left turn to Bessolles, go straight ahead, and follow the road when it swings left to emerge on to a main road, the D5.

Turn right for 250 metres, passing a lay-by, but taking a track which turns off left immediately after the crash barrier finishes. This track descends steeply through woodland, eventually emerging into the fields at the bottom of the hill. From here there is a fine view to the Château of Murol. Soon the track follows a stream, then crosses it, and emerges on to the main road again about one kilometre outside Murol. Turn left now, and follow the D5 to the edge of the town. Leave the road there by continuing forward when it makes a sharp swing to the left. At the next crossroads turn left to return to the start.

La Roche Romaine

Field Eryngium

Walk 20   The Monne Gorge

Map:	IGN 1:25000 2532 Ouest, Aydat & Saint-Nectaire
Time:	2$^1/_2$ hours walking
Grade:	Easy, apart from the stream crossing
Ascent:	200 metres

On this walk, what appears, on first acquaintance, to be an easy stroll, turns out to be rather more challenging. Olloix, where the walk begins, is about 6 kilometres north-east of Saint-Nectaire, and has an interesting history. The village is strung out along the side of a hill, on a south-facing slope, and was a principal possession of the Knights Hospitallers of Auvergne. They were soldier-monks, devoted to the care of pilgrims to the Holy Land, and their European establishments were extremely varied, part secular and part ecclesiastic. Of their Commandery at Olloix hardly anything survives, but the present parish church adjoins the site and part of it is contemporary. It contains the tomb of Prior Odon de Montaigut, head of the Hospitallers of Auvergne. Outside the church porch there is a medieval grave slab.

The Walk

Start from the parking space behind the chapel, near the road junction just west of Olloix.

Take the track leading north-west which, unusually, has English-type hedgerows of hawthorn, blackthorn, and briar, all the hedges full of small birds. Soon the view ahead opens towards Puy de Dôme and, in the foreground, the rocky slopes of the Monne Gorge. After passing a woodland area on the right, you reach an open viewpoint overlooking the gorge. Turn left down a wide track descending towards the river. This track swings right, then left, and as it approaches the river you will begin to hear the roar of water. After passing under power lines, take a right turn down a less-obvious path, which is waymarked in blue and runs parallel to the river, somewhat above it. Be sure to look out for a little meadow down on the left which has been an orchard at some time, and still has a few struggling fruit trees.

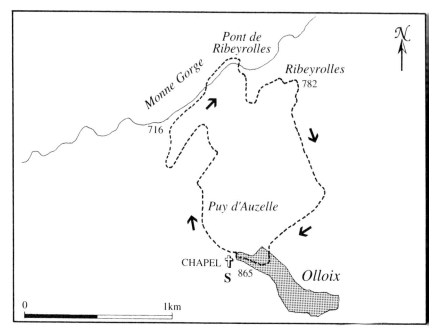

You can now hear the river close at hand, as it surges over the rocks, but only rarely do you get a glimpse of it as you descend, by way of a very narrow path, to river level. You now need to cross the river, and there is at this point a rather ramshackle footbridge. If it looks too frail there are other possibilities: one is to go a little further down stream, and jump across where the river narrows between two huge boulders, or, if that does not appeal to you either, you can go still further downstream, to the point where a large fir-tree trunk has fallen across the river and, being bare of branches, is easily straddled, allowing you to work your way across. Do not, however, attempt to get any further downstream on the south side, as the banks become very steep and slippery when wet.

Once across the stream, follow a level and clearly-defined path down, through masses of wild flowers in spring, to a surprisingly broad and well-built arched bridge at the Pont de Ribeyrolles. Cross the bridge and follow a clear track southwards. You pass the decayed ruins of what were once substantial houses, and are now almost lost in the trees. Presumably this was once the hamlet of Riberolles, to use its alternative spelling. At the top of the hill you reach an open plateau, with a cluster of rocks from which there is a view back into the gorge. At a junction of tracks fork right, crossing an open landscape of flower-filled meadows and pastures, dotted with large rocky outcrops. At

A gravestone at Olloix

the next junction turn right again, soon passing the cemetery and arriving at the edge of Olloix. Here, either go straight ahead, if you want to see the village and the church, or turn right and pass above the village to return more directly to the starting point.

Walk 21   Puy de Sancy

Maps:	IGN 1:25000 2432 Est, La Bourboule & Mont-Dore and 2433 Est, Egliseneuve d'Entraigues & Puy de Sancy
Time:	6 hours walking
Grade:	Difficult
Ascent:	920 metres

Puy de Sancy, the highest summit in the Massif Central at 1885 metres, is obviously a must in any book describing the walks in the area. But it is a rather overcrowded summit, because of the cable cars which go nearly to the top. The normal ascent from Le Mont-Dore is unshaded and tedious, but a much more pleasant approach can be made from a less popular side, by way of the Vallée de Chaudefour, which has been saved from commercial exploitation and nominated as a nature reserve. It is said to harbour *mouflons*, European wild sheep, though they are rarely seen.

The Walk

Start from the car park at Chambon des Neiges, at the end of the road west of Monneaux. This is equidistant from Saint-Nectaire and La Bourboule, being about 10 kilometres from either, but there is unfortunately no way of reaching it by public transport.

From the car park, walk up a small valley, turning left along a broad track just before the chair-lift station. When this stony track doubles back to the right, leave it by going forward on a green track over open heathland to reach another turning. Here the track again doubles back to the right, and once again you go forward on a smaller track that descends into woodland, following green waymarks. You now get a glimpse of the valley of Chaudefour, with Puy Ferrand at its head, before climbing over a ridge, with views back to the east, and descending to a fork. Take the upper, right-hand, fork and continue along the valley side to reach a point where a clearing in the trees permits a superb view of Puy Ferrand ahead. On joining a broader, more level, track, turn right, keeping above the road, and continue to climb and descend

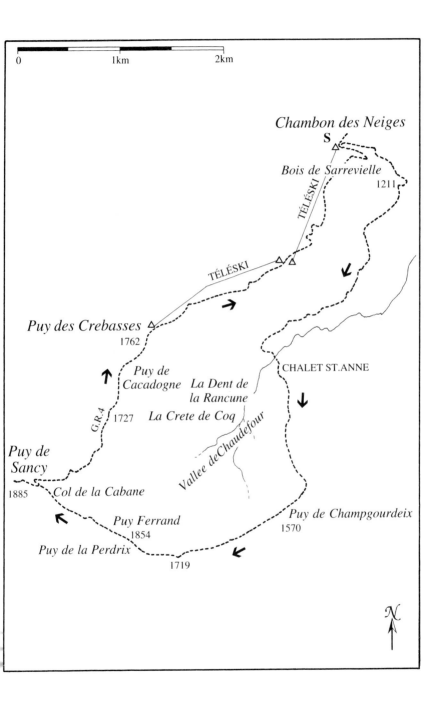

Chambon des Neiges
S
Bois de Sarrevielle
1211
TÉLÉSKI
TÉLÉSKI
Puy des Crebasses
1762
Puy de
Cacadogne
CHALET ST.ANNE
La Dent de
la Rancune
G.R.4
1727
La Crete de Coq
Vallee deChaudefour
Puy de
Sancy
1885
Col de la Cabane
Puy Ferrand
1854
Puy de Champgourdeix
1570
Puy de la Perdrix
1719
N

0   1km   2km

alternately until you cross a stile and arrive on another track very near to Chalet St Anne.

Turn left and cross a bridge, then go straight up the steep ridge ahead. The path, though waymarked (in green) is not very distinct at first, but becomes clearer as it climbs steeply through woodland. This section is marked *delicat* on IGN maps, suggesting that care is needed, but there are no special difficulties other than the uncompromising steepness. The track does, however, get you up very quickly, and has plentiful shade from the sun. In addition, when there is a break in the trees effort is rewarded by views, not only of Puy Ferrand, but also of the magnificent rock pinnacles of La Crete de Coq and La Dent de La Rancune, which offer formidable challenges to rock climbers. Once out of the trees, the going is much easier for a while, until a short climb takes you to a high plateau where alpine anemones grow in profusion. Here the track swings to the right: follow the skyline in that direction.

As the terminus for the cable car from Super Besse is approached, join a broad track descending from it. Half way up to the terminus turn right off the broad track and go along what soon becomes a narrow path with green waymarkers. This path rounds the north side of Puy de la Perdrix, and the south side of Puy Ferrand, and leads to an un-named summit which forms the terminus of the ski-tows from both north and south. It then descends to the Col de la Cabane. From here it is a short and not excessively steep climb to the summit of Puy de Sancy, where you will be rewarded, unless you are very unlucky, by a superlative view.

Return to the col and from the choice of paths offered, take the one signposted to the Col de la Croix St Robert. After a short descent, this rounds the east side of a green flat-topped hill, and continues to a col from where it climbs round the west side of Puy de Cacadogne. A short descent followed by a climb reaches the prominent ski tow on the Puy des Crebasses. Here you leave the main ridge by turning right and keeping to the right of the line of the ski-tow. Soon the path swings to the edge of the escarpment, giving splendid views, down to the right, into the upper valley of Chaudefour, whose circuit you have now completed.

After following the edge for a short distance, the path turns sharply left and descends to a little plateau, where the lower station of the ski-tow and the upper station of the chair lift are situated. Pass between the two, and turn right along a track. Soon after passing under the chair lift, leave the track by turning left down a steep zig-zag route close to the lift pylons. On reaching the intermediate station of the chair lift, you will need to take the level track going forward more or less parallel to the line of the lift, since the original line

Puy Ferrand

of the footpath, dropping into the bottom of the valley, has been obliterated by ski-ing developments. By taking the first turning on the left, you will arrive at the foot of the chair lift, where a right turn leads you quickly back to the car park.

Besse-en-Chandesse

Besse was a medieval walled town, built on a steep hillside above the Pavin river west of Issoire. Although only a fragment now remains of its walls, one of the former gates has survived, surmounted by a 15th century bell tower, which is a prominent feature of the town. The importance of the place was due to its situation, on the route to a high pass between the valleys of the Allier and the Dordogne. Its location made its market pre-eminent in the district, and a cheese market is still held on Mondays. It was the market which persuaded merchants to settle there, and many of the 16th and 17th century houses that remain were built by them.

The town centre has retained its medieval plan, with numerous narrow streets and alleys. Guided tours, lasting $1^1/_2$ hours, start from the Tourist Office on Wednesday and Thursday afternoons during the summer, or you can wander around at your leisure. Things to look out for, in addition to the bell tower and a few towered staircases which you can hardly miss, include the Château du Baillie (the residence of the town's principal officer), a royal residence – probably used only occasionally, when the retinue was in the district, the narrow paved Shambles called La Bouchèrie – and the church.

Within the church, the nave and transept are 12th century and retain some fine carved capitals even better than those at Saint-Nectaire and Orcival. Surprisingly, an apsidial chapel was added in 1822, after the French Revolution. It was built for a special purpose, though, to house the statue of Notre Dame de Vassivière, whose processional transfer in early summer and autumn is described in Walk 26.

There is an enormous range of accommodation available in the town of Besse and its immediate surroundings. With one three star hotel, the Mouflons, seven two star hotels, and numerous one star hotels in the town or nearby villages, it is difficult to know where to start. There are also *gîtes*, apartments, rooms to let and a municipal camp site.

This all sounds excellent, but the camp site does not open until the middle of June – nor do any of the others in the immediate locality – and the accommodation other than in the large hotels is very hit and miss until the French holiday season starts in July. This is hardly surprising, given that foreign visitors form only a very small proportion of those who stay in Besse, but it is pleasing to be able to report that the Tourist Office is open from early May, and is extremely helpful, both in providing information and in finding accommodation for chance visitors of all nationalities.

Walk 22   The Neighbourhood of Besse

Map:	IGN 1:25000 2533 Ouest, Besse-en-Chandesse
Time:	2 hours walking
Grade:	Easy
Ascent:	110 metres

A short and easy walk, which begins by threading the streets of the old town, before making a circuit using the local paths.

The Walk

Start from the Tourist Information Office in the old town.

Emerging from the Tourist Office, turn right, then immediately left, and walk along Rue Merciere, the Haberdasher's street, into the Place de la Gayme. Now keep straight ahead into the Rue du Marche. Take the first turn on the right, then go immediately left and cross the road to reach another signposted to Compains. Cross the Besse by-pass, and take the right-hand of the two roads opposite, with the La Gazelle hotel on your right. Go straight across at the crossroads, along the lane signposted to La Charreyre. The metalled surface finishes shortly, at La Charreyre farm, but you continue along what is now a sandy track, passing another of the ubiquitous wayside Crosses which have survived in such numbers in this area.

The meadows to either side have obviously been kept free from herbicides, as they display not only the usual meadow flowers, but also cowslips in large numbers and masses of white narcissus in May. The Cranesbills, too, are prolific, particularly a very pale Woody form which, like its relative the Bloody Cranesbill, contains tannins in its roots which were formerly used to staunch wounds. This use gave rise to the name of the common form of the flower, the name having nothing to do with its reddish colour.

Ignoring a turning to the right, continue uphill. On this section be sure to turn to view the panorama unfolding behind you. On reaching a metalled lane, turn right for 250 metres, then go sharply back to the left, along the road to Chandèze. In spite of the change in spelling, this is recognizably the same name as that associated with Besse in the full form of its name. Besse-en-

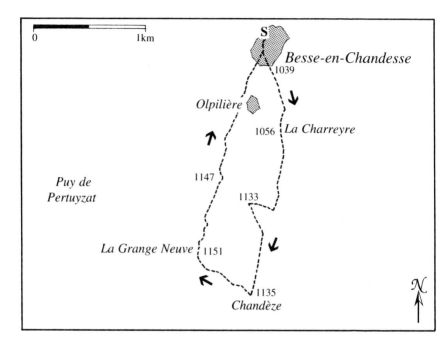

Chandesse, and one wonders how such a tiny village came to be linked to an important market town. At the fork in the road where the village begins, take neither branch (!), turning right instead to go along a sandy track which climbs to a plateau.

On reaching a junction of four tracks, turn right, down to the farm of La Grange Neuve, where the track becomes a metalled road. Continue along it, ignoring a turning coming in from the right, but noting an inscribed Cross base on the left just before, which is perched incongruously, and rather precariously, on three small stones. As you descend, the volcanic cone of Puy de Pertuyzat is a prominent feature on your left. The route soon reaches the outskirts of the village of Olpilière: turn left down a grassy track just before the first house. This easy track leads directly towards Besse, and brings you out between the sports ground and the sports centre on to the by-pass which encircles the old town. Go straight across and down the street to the bell tower, turning left and immediately right to pass under its archway, to emerge into the Place de la Gayme. From there, return to the Tourist Office by way of the Rue Merciere.

Walk 23   The Pavin and Vaucoux Rivers

Map:	IGN 1:25000 2533 Ouest, Besse-en-Chandesse
Time:	4 hours walking
Grade:	Moderate
Ascent:	240 metres

This route is described as starting and finishing at Besse, which is where most people will stay, or start the walk. But the mid-point of the route lies 240 metres below Besse in a deep river valley, so anyone who feels strongly that a descent followed by an ascent is the wrong way to do a walk, and has their own transport, could park at Ourcière and make the circuit from there.

The Walk

Start from the parish church in the old town of Besse, which has a number of car parks.

From the parish church, turn east, down the old road to Clermont. After 150 metres, when the road swings left, turn right down a lane, and when the lane itself turns sharply left, turn right again, along a walled track. This quickly brings you to the road at Le Rif. Turn left to reach a road junction after 100 metres. Go straight across the D149 into the lane opposite, signposted to Thiaulaire, but after 200 metres leave it by turning left along a gravelled track. Follow the track, ignoring two turnings to the left, past shady woodland to reach the first house in Thiaulaire. Turn left there on to a track that descends, with a fine view of the Pic de St Pierre ahead, before entering woods. At the first junction, turn sharply back to the right, continuing to descend through woodland. At the bottom of the first clearing, when the main track bends sharply back to the left, turn right up a short slope to follow another track beside a wall that goes into beech woods.

Halfway down the hill, a deep hollow way, previously visible down to the left, joins your track from the left: continue down a broad terrace that is deep in leaf mould, except when scoured away by thunderstorms, as happened when I was last there. The track meanders pleasantly above the stream – which is in fact the Pavin, whose source in Lac Pavin is described in Walk 24

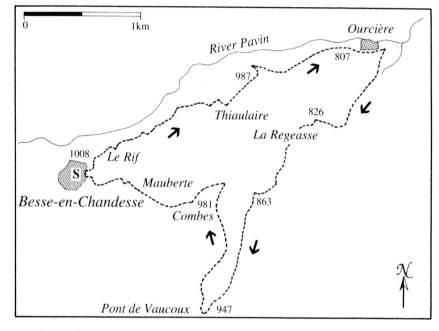

– before descending to the village of Ourcière. Turn right at the crucifix, next to which is an old, single-storey building roofed with *lauzes*, the local rough slates. Remarkably, it is windowless, though it has a chimney and a nicely-moulded doorway. It bears a distinct resemblance to a chapel seen later in the walk, and may perhaps have once been a chapel, but was deconsecrated and converted to a cottage with a chimney.

After turning right here, it is no more than 100 metres to the next turn. Fork right, only to make yet another right turn after a few paces, when a road comes in from the left. The road now takes you along a narrow valley to a bridge. Cross the bridge, beyond which the road becomes a stony track climbing gently by the side of the Vaucoux. Turn left at the next fork, by the clearing of La Regeasse, and climb above the stream. When a meadow is reached, skirt around it on the left, instead of going straight across the middle, as shown on the IGN map. The way is steep now, and goes through tall, slender, beeches, before joining a level track which is followed to the right.

The track reaches a road at the bridge of Vaucoux. Turn right over the bridge and follow the road for 200 metres. Just after the farm, a track descends on your right: follow it down to a stream crossing, ignoring a track going back on the right immediately beforehand. After crossing, ascend the hill to reach a plateau with a fine view of Besse and the surrounding hills. On joining a

The Falls of Vaucoux

stony track, turn left along it, to reach, after 400 metres, a road by the tiny chapel of Combes, a chapel that bears a strong resemblance to the windowless building at Ourcière. Turn right along the road, then go right again after 100 metres. Now just before this latter road terminates at the farm of Mauberte, take a left turn along a gravelled track, going past a wayside Cross. You quickly reach a metalled road: go straight across it, into the small field opposite and follow the right-hand wall. This wall guides you to the main road where, once again, you go straight across, heading for the car park by the cemetery of Besse. Turn right here to return to the starting point at the parish church.

Walk 24   Lac Pavin

Map:	IGN 1:25000 2533 Ouest, Besse-en-Chandesse
Time:	$5^1/_2$ hours walking
Grade:	Moderate
Ascent:	400 metres (including Montchal)

Quite a long walk, but not a particularly energetic one, for the only real climbing to be done is the optional detour to the top of Puy de Montchal.

The Walk

Start from the Tourist Information Office in the centre of Besse-en-Chandesse.

Emerging again from the Tourist Office, turn right and take the first turn on the left into Rue Merciere, which leads into the Place de la Gayme. Turn right now, under the archway of the bell tower, turning right and immediately left as you emerge. Walk up the street beyond to the by-pass. Go straight across, passing to the right of the sports hall, and following a green track which goes gently uphill below the new houses on your left. On reaching the road just south of Olpilière, turn right and climb the hill, ignoring a track going off to the right, to reach a fork in the road. Bear right and follow this metalled road, (past the Cross base mentioned on Walk 22) to reach the farm of La Grange Neuve where the metalled surface finishes. Continue forward on a sandy track to reach a junction. Turn right for 200 metres before the track turns sharply left to recover its former direction.

The way now leads up to a high cow pasture, where the only sound is of cowbells and skylarks, and where there is an expansive view forward. Ignoring a turning to the right, continue for $1^1/_2$ kilometres to join a road. Turn right along it and skirt a deep valley, clothed in beech woods, to the left. At the road junction, with its inevitable Cross, keep right, following the road towards the forested Puy de Montchal. Pass a turning on the right, and one on the left. Then, when you arrive at a point 50 metres short of the Regional Park signboard – which advises you that Lac Pavin is the youngest volcanic crater in France (a mere 5,800 years old) – you turn left.

Follow the path high above the lake, though screened from it by trees, and

108

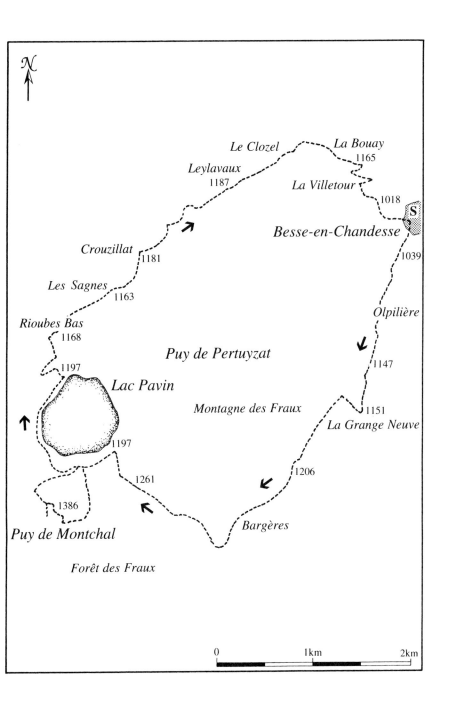

N

Le Clozel
La Bouay
1165

Leylavaux
1187
La Villetour
1018

S

Besse-en-Chandesse

Crouzillat
1181
1039

Les Sagnes
1163

Olpilière

Rioubes Bas
1168

1147

1197
Puy de Pertuyzat

Lac Pavin
1151
La Grange Neuve

Montagne des Fraux

1197
1206

1261

Bargères

1386

Puy de Montchal

Forêt des Fraux

0   1km   2km

turn right at the next junction. Go right again immediately if you want to descend to the lake. If, on the other hand, you want to climb the Puy first, keep left at this second turning and follow a broad track around its base, before turning left up a smaller, waymarked path to the summit. You can either turn right at the top to view the panorama, and then return by the same route, or you can turn left and descend steeply through woodland into the grassy bowl of the crater – surely the oddest place to find masses of wild daffodils growing. This path, having brought you down from the highest part of the crater rim, now takes you out over the lower lip, and you quickly find yourself on a broad track. Go straight ahead at the junction, and you soon arrive back at the starting point for the climb to the Puy.

Whichever route you took, you now descend by a delightful path to the west side of Lac Pavin. The lake is a mecca for anglers, and is the legendary site of the original town of Besse, which was swallowed by the waters in an act of divine retribution, and whose submerged bells can still be heard at certain times. There is a useful restaurant here, rather more than half way through the walk. On leaving it, take the road to the left, pausing to look at the dramatic descent of the stream flowing out of the lake, whose waters we saw further downstream on the previous walk.

Cross the D978 at the garage, going along the road opposite and leaving it after 100 metres to turn right across the D149. The lane opposite climbs uphill towards Rioubes, but after only another 100 metres you turn right towards Les Sagnes. Just before reaching the house, where the road ends, turn left along the fence. Pass behind the barn and take the green track climbing the bank ahead. It is easily followed at first, being a clear track past clumps of pale narcissi and darker daffodils, but after crossing a fence the path becomes less clear, though it is still indicated by red and white waymarkers on prominent stones. Go over a stile to join the farm road at Crouzillat, and turn right along it. Go left after 100 metres and follow a road as it twists its way round a hairpin bend and climbs to a road junction from where there is a fine view down to Besse.

Take the right turn here, signposted to Leylavaux, walking through that hamlet, and on past Le Clozel and La Bouay. About 500 metres after leaving La Bouay you leave the road. The turning you are looking for is a stony path off to the right, and is almost opposite another turning to the left. The path zig-zags down to La Villetour where you turn left. On arriving at the water trough turn right, to cross the bridge. Now go left, and finally right at the crossroads to return to Besse town centre.

Walk 25   Compains and Montcineyre

Map:	IGN 1:25000 2533 Ouest, Besse-en Chandesse
Time:	4 hours walking
Grade:	Moderate
Ascent:	330 metres (including Montcineyre)

Compains, like Besse, is about 1,000 metres above sea level, so that only moderate climbing is involved in this walk, which is almost entirely on good paths. There is a variety of interest too, for as well as the attractive country through which the path passes, there is a little known 12th century chapel, a very beautiful lake, and the extinct volcano of Montcineyre.

The Walk

Start from the church in the centre of Compains. The village lies about 12 kilometres south of Besse, on the D36.

From the church, take the road heading east (the D26, towards Issoire), but turn off it almost immediately to the left, along the minor road signposted to St Anastaise. After less than a kilometre the road makes a hairpin bend to the right: leave it at this point by turning left into a hedged green lane going up the valley. After about 50 metres a stream crossing is reached. This can be tricky after prolonged rain, but at other times presents no difficulty. The way is now broad and easy, as it climbs through shady woodland on the east side of the valley. On emerging into the fields at the top, there are three wire fences to be negotiated in quick succession, but none of them are difficult, and you quickly find yourself at the surprisingly remote – but quite delightful – 12th century chapel of Saint Gorgon.

The dedication is to a 3rd century saint martyred in the reign of the Roman Emperor, Diocletian. A statue from the chapel is kept locally, and can be seen on application, but the relics are in the Presbytère in Besse. Though the design and the original structure of the chapel are 12th century, its general condition is so good as to make it quite certain that there has been extensive rebuilding. In fact this has been carried out twice at least, once in the 19th century, and again very recently, and it is evident that someone keeps an eye

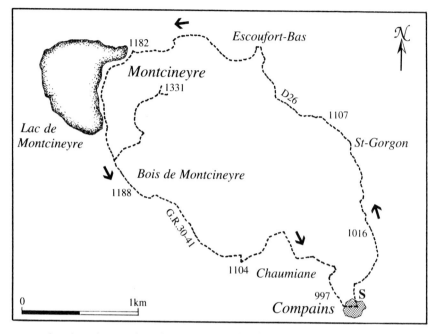

on the chapel even though it is now used only by nesting birds. Its circular form is very unusual, but the design as a whole is plain and unornamented, with window openings, but no attempt at glazing.

Leave the chapel along the rather overgrown green lane which may once have been an important route, with the chapel sited beside it, following it to reach a farm road. Turn left to reach the main road. Now turn right for nearly a kilometre, and take the first turning on the left, a broad gravelled track that winds around the base of Montcineyre and leads to a lake which has no outlet. As you continue round the eastern side of the lake you will notice, on your left, evidence of a considerable recent landslide on the steep slopes of the mountain, while to your right are the unmistakeable signs of ancient woodland management in a group of magnificent coppiced beeches. Coppicing appears to have been widely practised hereabouts, massive beech stools being seen in the woods right up to the rim of the former volcano.

About 300 metres after leaving the southern tip of the lake, turn left along a minor track, joining the main track from the left. Soon you will see a building over on your left, before the track passes through a wire fence in a little clearing and climbs through a dense fir plantation. Some 400 metres after taking this minor track you need to look out for an unmarked track on your left, just short of the point where you can see down into a deep crater

Saint Gorgon

on the left. Turn left along this track, and after a few paces take the left-hand (upper) track of the two going forward. Climb through thick beech woods, with the crater down on your right. Higher up the woodland becomes thinner and more mixed, and you find yourself on a narrow ridge, for although the lower crater is still on the right, an upper crater has now appeared on the left. When the path forks you can either go right, to a point on the southern rim where there is an excellent view to the south, or go left along a path which cuts across to the highest point, where the view is more restricted because of recent planting.

In either event retrace your steps, remembering to take the two right turns in quick succession on the way down, to arrive back at the base of the hill near the southern end of the lake. Now turn left, heading south, to reach a fork in the track, where you keep to the left. Continue past a farm on the right to join a metalled road near the hamlet of Chaumiane. Turn right here for 50 metres, then go left along a track which contours above the valley with views down to Compains below. The track now crosses a low ridge: where you leave it by turning right, through beech woods, and descend steeply following red and white waymarkers. At the foot of the hill, the waymarkers guide you first left, then right into a deep, walled, hollow way. Soon, the church steeple appears ahead and the way reaches a road. Turn right into the village.

113

Walk 26   Lac Chauvet and Vassivière

Map:	IGN 1:25000 2433 Est, Egliseneuve-d'Entraigues
Time:	4 hours walking
Grade:	Easy
Ascent:	100 metres

An easy walk with virtually no climbing, which links two very different attractions a few kilometres to the west of Besse – a beautiful lake, and a popular pilgrimage chapel.

The Walk

Start from the lakeside at Lac Chauvet, where the minor road linking it to the D203 ends, and car parking is possible. Though this is described as a circular walk, it would obviously be possible to finish at Vassivière to avoid retracing one's steps, if transport could be arranged.

Turning away from the lake, head west along a broad track for 100 metres before making a left turn at a footpath signposted to Pont de Clamouze. The path passes through very open woodland where there is no obvious line to follow, but soon becomes a definite track through thicker woods. The path is about 100 metres from the shoreline, though the lake itself is out of sight beyond the trees. After crossing a small stream, the woodland again becomes very open: go through a fence and leave the wood into open pasture. This is not the usual French pasture though, for the scattered trees include a number similar in appearance to copper beeches, giving the landscape the appearance of parkland. The wild-flowers here are excellent, and include masses of yellow gentians. This distinctly odd plant does not flower until it is 10 years old, at least, but from then produces about 10,000 seeds every season.

There is no clear path across this open area, so walk eastwards to reach a cross fence somewhere near the point where the long distance footpath from Egliseneuve comes through it. Turn left, ie northwards, along a clear path, with good views of the Sancy massif ahead. The path becomes a broad track and leads through hay meadows to the road west of the Pont de Clamouze.

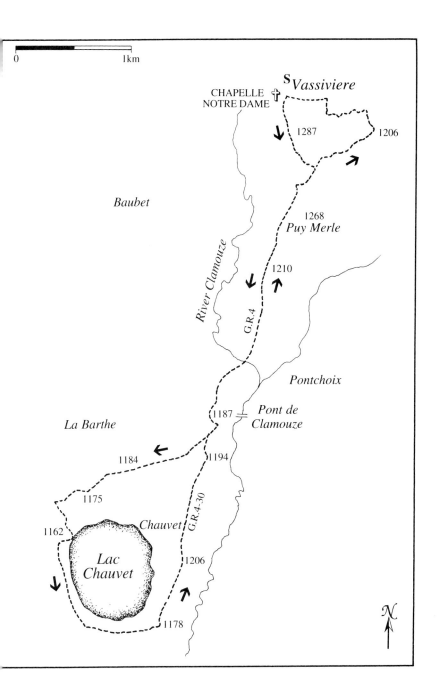

Turn right along the road for 100 metres, then go left, then right again after another 100 metres. Now follow this farm road, signposted to Puy-Merle, until, just before reaching the farm, you turn left over a stile at a white and red waymarker. The next section can be a little wet after rain as there are several small streams to cross but, after crossing another stile, drier ground is reached. Head up on to the crest of a ridge, reaching it at a small nick in the skyline. The ridge is the home of many small birds, and there may be buzzards overhead. Ahead now the chapel of Vassivière, the next destination, is prominent. The path to it, though it is indistinct just here, can be seen as a clear track through the conifer plantation ahead. Once into the woods, the track is broad and there are no turnings until, emerging from the wood, you arrive at a metalled lane. Turn right for 200 metres to reach a road junction., Turn right again, descending the hill towards the main road, but perhaps averting your eyes from the wholly insensitive siting of the ski-village of Super Besse, starkly in view on the hill ahead.

Just before reaching the main road, turn left through the fence and follow the winding track upwards past twelve Crucifixes on the way to the hillside chapel of Vassivière. Presumably, the chapel was built originally to serve the keepers of the flocks and herds of Besse, who spent the summer on these high pastures. Each summer a statue of the Virgin is taken from the church of Besse, in solemn procession, for eight kilometres to Vassivière, and returned in autumn. This ancient custom takes place on the first Sunday in July for the outward procession, the return procession being at the end of September. The September procession is followed by a celebration in the town.

After visiting the shrine, turn left along the metalled lane and follow it as far as the first junction. Turn right and follow a lane for 200 metres, then turn left into the conifer plantation. The track, which was used on the outward route, will take you back to the grassy ridge, which you follow towards Puy-Merle, remembering to swing right across the stiles to join the road just west of the farm. Now retrace your steps to the main road, turning right when you reach it and following it for 100 metres. You now have the choice of following it for a further $1^1/_2$ kilometres, to the turn for Lac Chauvet, but if the road is busy you may prefer to follow your outward route southwards around the lake. Alternatively, though no path is marked on the IGN map, French rambling parties sometimes leave the track southward after the fence at the top of the hill, and follow the northern edge of the lake back to the parking area.

Orcival

The names of Orcival and Saint-Nectaire are sometimes linked, because of the similarity – both in style and date – of their Romanesque churches. Yet though both villages are small, and both are dominated by their churches, the similarity ceases there, for their settings are quite dissimilar. Orcival lies low down, rather hidden in the valley of the Sioulet, whereas Saint-Nectaire, as we have seen, sits on a hill top and is clearly visible.

The two churches, of comparable 12th century date, are built in the distinctive Auvergnat style, for which the prototype is said to have been Notre-Dame-du-Port at Clermont-Ferrand, though the church at Issoire and that at Saint-Saturnin also contribute to the theme. What strikes the visitor is the scale of the building and the splendid assembly at the east end, with chapels radiating from an ambulatory, a particular feature of pilgrimage churches on which the Auvergnat style is partly based.

On more detailed examination, it is the richness of carving on the column capitals which impresses, though there are differences here in that religious themes predominate at Saint-Nectaire, while Orcival inclines to naturalistic ornament. The latter church was founded by the monks of La Chaise Dieu, who were responsible for no less than 100 churches in the locality, and who were evidently patrons rather than participating in the building themselves.

Orcival, like Besse, has its religious procession, though here it takes place by torchlight at the Feast of the Ascension. The statue of the Virgin carried at Orcival is of comparable date to the church itself, but the procession goes only as far as the local hilltop, the route being followed in the first walk described from the village.

Though no more than a village, Orcival has a two-star hotel, the Roche: four one-star hotels, L'Ajasserie d'Orcival, Les Bourelles, Notre-Dame, and Au Vieux Logis, and other accommodation as well as several restaurants. There is no organised camp site in the village, the nearest being at Flechat, 5 kilometres away by road, but *Camping de la Ferme* is available at Les Planchettes, $1^1/_2$ kilometres south of the village, where Saint-Nectaire cheese, and other farm products, are made and sold.

Walk 27   The Neighbourhood of Orcival

Map:	IGN 1:25000 2432 Est, La Bourboule & Mont-Dore
Time:	2 hours walking
Grade:	Easy
Ascent:	180 metres

An easy walk exploring the country close to Orcival, with good views of the Chaîne des Puys.

The Walk

Start from the village square of Orcival, by the church.

Leave the square in the middle of the village along the street directly facing the east end of the church, following it to the by-pass. There are two lanes opposite: take the right-hand one, signposted to Chapelle Notre Dame, and climb up to this delightful, classically-inspired, sanctuary chapel. There is a good view down to the village and church of Orcival from here, and it is easy to appreciate just how well the 12th century Romanesque style of the mother church fits into its urban setting, while the totally different 18th century style of the daughter chapel is equally right for its rural background.

From the chapel take the level track heading north, quickly arriving at the road. Turn right for 100 metres, passing the farm of La Croix, then fork right up a broad track. Ignore a turn back to the right to reach a point from which there is a good, though rather distant, view of the Château of Cordès, with its formal hedged gardens by Le Nôtre. The château was built between the 13th and 15th centuries, and is considered to be one of the most attractive country houses in France, though it is rather small to be called a château. It is well worth a visit while you are in the area. Shortly after the viewpoint fork right and climb to another, with a view to the north-east which takes in the whole of the Chaîne des Puys with Puy de Dôme itself as the centre point.

The track now starts to descend: turn off to the right along a grassy track, hedged on both sides, between meadows. This fine almost level track which, unaccountably, is not shown on even the largest scale IGN maps, leads into

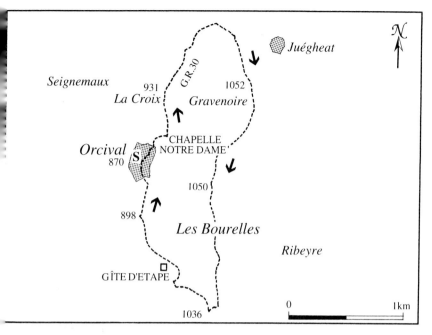

shady beech woods and, after about 600 metres, joins another, climbing up from Juégheat. Turn right along the new track which leads to the summit plateau of Gravenoire. Here a green track comes in from the right, while the track you are on swings left. After a further 200 metres another junction is reached: turn left again, heading due south now on a pleasant level track through tall pines which, it must be admitted, do obscure the view.

At a junction of routes go straight ahead, still heading south along the principal track, which soon starts to descend. As you emerge from the trees there is a clear view ahead, with the Puy de l'Ouire as the most prominent feature. On reaching the road (the D74) at its highest point, turn right for 100 metres, then go right again and follow a track downhill. Keeping straight ahead at the first junction, the track now bends to the right and the gradient steepens. Take the left fork at next junction to arrive at a farm where the road begins. Follow the road downhill back to Orcival.

Walk 28   Roche Branlante

Map:	IGN 1:25000 2432 Est, La Bourboule & Mont-Dore
Time:	$2^1/_2$ hours walking
Grade:	Easy
Ascent:	210 metres

An easy half-day's walk in gentle, rolling, countryside, with extensive views.

The Walk

Start from the village square and car park in Orcival.

Leave Orcival along the track climbing up behind the war memorial, on the south side of the church. The track is signposted to the Tombeau de la Vierge, the Orientation Table, and the Roche Branlante, which the route visits in that order. The track climbs steeply past one of the numerous round-towered houses which are a feature of Orcival, but can also be seen in other places in the Auvergne. As you ascend, by the route used by the annual torchlight procession, going past fifteen Crucifixes, there is no shortage of opportunities to stop and take in the view back down to the village. Eventually, the track arrives at the Virgin's shrine.

Immediately beyond the shrine the route joins a road at a hairpin bend. Go straight ahead, up the hill, with good views of the delightful valley to your left. After passing the tiny hamlet of Chamberte, the road doubles back to the right: continue to follow it up to the quarry at the top of the hill, beyond which you join another road (the D74). Turn left along the road to reach, after about $^1/_2$ kilometre, at the orientation table, an excellent viewpoint, with the view eastwards extending to the Puy de Dôme and its associated hills. Continue along the road to a fork and keep to the right on the way signposted to the Roche Branlante. After a further 400 metres turn right again, at a similar sign.

The track follows the edge of the woods, where there are numerous red squirrels. Where the track starts heading downhill towards the village of Soussat, turn off left, as indicated, once again, by a sign. The path is now a

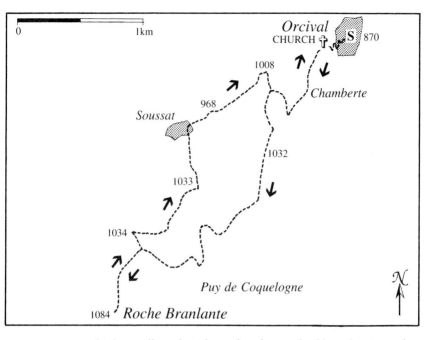

Orcival
CHURCH ✝ S 870

1008

968

Soussat

Chamberte

1032

1033

1034

Puy de Coquelogne

1084 Roche Branlante

0   1km

N

grassy one, and is less well-used, with an abundance of wild raspberries and brambles. Cross a small dingle and descend a little before resuming the gentle climb. Now, just when you thought you had arrived at your destination, the path turns disconcertingly downhill towards Rochefort. Before long, however, another sign to Roche Branlante points back up the slope to the left, and this time you do actually arrive at the rock.

Roche Branlante turns out to be a cluster of rocks which includes one huge perched boulder, probably deposited by melting ice. Overall, however, the site is a little disappointing in view of all the local publicity. As a viewpoint, it is good, however, much of the valley running down to Rochefort Montagne being revealed, though, unfortunately, the upper valley, under the cliffs of Roche Tuilière and Roche Sanadoire, remains hidden. To return to Orcival, follow the outward path back for $^1/_2$ kilometre to the last turning, but then turn left, downhill, for 200 metres into a gorse-filled waste. On reaching a fence, turn right, along a clear track between two wire fences, which takes you across a stream and on to a low ridge.

On the crest of the ridge, there is a junction of tracks. Turn left, heading directly for the tree-crowned summit of Puy d'Ebert. When this main track swings to the left, leave it by turning right down a stony track, which maintains the original direction towards the hamlet of Soussat. On arriving

Haymaking at Soussat

at the road serving the hamlet, turn right and follow it to the main road. Turn right again, and follow the main road past two left turns to reach a third, signposted to Chamberte. Take this turning, going past a quarry and downhill to the right. Continue back to the left past Chamberte and, at a hairpin bend, leave the road and follow the steep path down past the shrine, retracing your outward route back to the start.

Walk 29   Les Cheires Hautes

Map:	IGN 1:25000 2532 Ouest, Aydat & Saint-Nectaire
Time:	$2^1/_2$ hours walking
Grade:	Easy
Ascent:	50 metres

Les Cheires Hautes is the name given to an area 10 kilometres due east of Orcival, created by lava flows spilled from the craters of Puy de la Vache and Puy de Lassolas. It now supports a cover of juniper, birch, and pines which make up a most attractive open woodland. This easy walk follows a path through the heart of this area, visiting the craters of the well-known volcanoes.

The Walk

Start from the car park of the Château de Montlosier, the headquarters of the *Parc des Volcans*, where the exhibition showing the main features of the volcanic region of the Auvergne is well worth seeing.

Leave the car park by the southern exit, crossing the road and following the broad track heading south. Almost immediately, you pass a very attractive little lake on your left. Continue along a level path which meanders between woodland and meadow. Soon, the path starts to climb, very gently, through the mixed birch and pine woods typical of the area, and then goes around the base of the Puy de Vichatel to reach the main road.

Cross to find a little path, almost opposite, which disappears into the trees to the left. This path quickly turns south, along the woodland boundary fence, and leads to a broader track. Turn left along this track to reach the Col de la Ventouse. At this major road junction you again cross the road, this time by way of the thoughtfully provided pedestrian crossing, and climb the new flight of wooden steps opposite. Now turn right along a track that heads south, staying well above the road at first, but soon turning away from it into the woods where the traffic noise is soon lost.

At a junction, where a new track turns off right and descends to the main

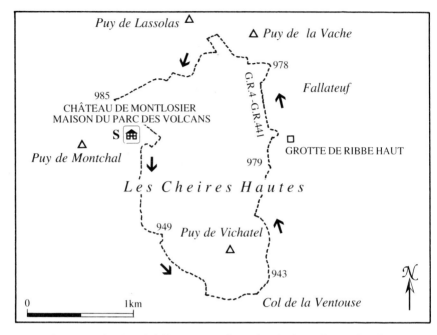

Puy de Lassolas

Puy de la Vache

978

985

Fallateuf

CHÂTEAU DE MONTLOSIER
MAISON DU PARC DES VOLCANS

G.R.4-G.R.441

S 🏠

GROTTE DE RIBBE HAUT

Puy de Montchal

979

Les Cheires Hautes

949 Puy de Vichatel

943

0   1km

Col de la Ventouse

N

road, go straight ahead, following a well-used path through woodland on the eastern side of Puy de Vichatel. Almost imperceptibly the vegetation changes, as Les Cheires Hautes, with its more open woods and more diverse species, is reached. In addition to pine and beech, which are commonplace in woodlands throughout the Auvergne, there is birch and hazel, willow and bird-cherry, together with a rich ground cover of wild flowers. The path traverses this area for $1^1/_2$ kilometres before reaching a road (the D5). Turn right for 200 metres to reach an open clearing used as a car park.

Ignoring the track to the left immediately before the car park, take, instead, the next turning on the left, a broad track ascending from the clearing, which, after about 200 metres, leads you to the scene of the volcanic outpourings of Puy de la Vache. This is a strange area, once quarried to reveal the red volcanic ash and lumps of lava which underlie the whole of Les Cheires Hautes and help to explain its distinctive vegetation. Cross this quarried area, heading west, to reach a flight of steps leading up to a short section of woodland path, which is followed by another flight of steps leading down into the crater of Puy de la Vache.

The crater floor, perhaps surprisingly, turns out to be a grassy clearing, though overhung by the soil-less slopes of the volcano's rim. At the southern extremity of the clearing there is a broad track running north-west to south-

The lakeside near Montlosier

east. Turn right along it for a few hundred metres into the crater of the sister volcano of Puy de Lassolas. Now retrace your steps along the broad track, but this time go past the first crater, as far as a none-too-obvious junction. Turn back to the right on what soon becomes a clear and well-maintained track. On arriving at a crossways turn left on to a track that is followed to reach a road about 100 metres from the entrance to the car park of the Château de Montlosier.

Walk 30   The Chaîne des Puys

Map:	IGN 1:25000 2531 Est, Clermont Ferrand et Puy de Dôme
Time:	6 hours walking
Grade:	Moderate
Ascent:	500 metres

A fairly long walk, but without any difficulties, which visits three quite different volcanic peaks of the Chaîne des Puys.

The Walk

Start from the railway station at Le Vauriat, on the D941, 16 kilometres north-west of Clermont-Ferrand. Le Vauriat is easily accessible from various centres by either road or rail.

Start from the station car park, turning left as you leave it to reach the D941 at the level crossing. Cross the railway and turn right immediately, towards Le Bouchet. At the edge of the village, take a farm track on the left (a red and white waymarked long distance footpath), then take the second path on the right, which skirts the houses of Le Bouchet. Turn left when another green track comes in from the right, then left again almost immediately at a crossways. This green lane continues to a fork: take the right branch and follow it until it joins a broad gravelled track. Here, turn left into Beauregard.

Keep left up the village street, turning right at the top along a shady farm track. Continue for $1^1/_2$ kilometres, ignoring a turning to the right and one to the left. Then, on reaching the top of a low ridge, turn left at a crossways. After 500 metres turn right, then left after a further 200 metres, at the far edge of the plantation on your left. Now climb up, ignoring three turnings on your left, the second of which you will return to a little later, to reach the foot of Puy Chopine. Here, turn left along a level track for 300 metres, then take a right turn for the climb to the peak. Although the summit is tree-clothed, the climb is worthwhile for the views to all points of the compass, which you will take in as you make a circuit of its almost-conical mass on the way to the top. The peak is not quite what it appears, however, for it consists not of volcanic

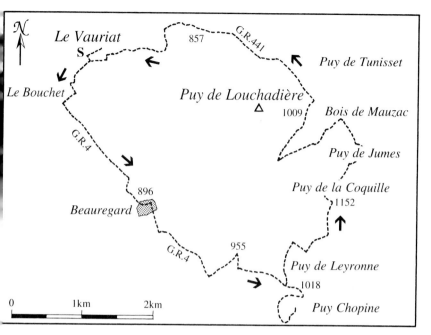

ash but of granite which apparently stuck in the throat of the volcano and was exposed at a much later date by erosion of the volcanic cone.

From Puy Chopine, descend by the outward route to reach the path junction noted on the way up. Fork right along another long-distance footpath signposted to Volvic. This path skirts the little Puy de Leyronne on the west, then swings back sharply to the right before making a left turn downhill for a short distance to reach the col between that summit and the Puy de la Coquille. At the col, ignore the broad track ahead, which leads towards the Puy de Louchadière, and turn to the right up a rather overgrown little path leading to the ridge. Now follow the ridge to the rounded summit of exposed volcanic ash. From here there is an extensive view to the south, encompassing not only the nearby Puy Chopine but the whole chain of volcanoes, including the deeply-cratered Puy Pariou and the prominent mass of Puy de Dôme. From Puy de la Coquille, turn west down the red and white waymarked path before turning north-east again to climb to the perfectly-preserved rim of the Puy de Jumes.

This crater turns out to be well-vegetated, mainly heather with a scattering of small trees and bushes. After half-circling the rim leave, northward, from the lowest point and descend towards the quarries. Turn left on reaching the main track at the bottom. Fork right after 400 metres, and continue until you

The Chaîne des Puys

reach a low ridge running south from Puy de Louchadière. At this point you must double back to the right at a waymarked tree. The track climbs gently, then descends towards the quarries. Turn left along the quarry access road and keep left to reach the main road (the D941) after about one kilometre. Cross the road and take the track running parallel to it, on its north side, heading west. This track gradually swings away from the road and, after one kilometre, is joined by a track coming in from the north. Continue heading west but, 100 metres before the track crosses the railway, take the green path to the left. This path heads south, then west, through woodland to reach the main road at Le Vauriat just short of the level crossing where the walk began.